FASTING   FASTING

FASTING

FAST ING

FAST ING

FAST ING

Christ did not say "if you fast" …
but rather, "When you fast" …

FASTING   FASTING

Romara Dean
Chatham

Bridge-Logos *Publishers*

North Brunswick, New Jersey 08902 USA

Scripture references are taken from the King James
Version of the Bible, unless otherwise identified.

FASTING
by Romara Dean Chatham
Copyright © 1987 by Bridge-Logos Publishers
Reprinted 1999
Library of Congress Catalog Card Number: 85-73212
International Standard Book Number: 0-88270-604-7

Published by:
Bridge-Logos *Publishers*
1300 Airport Road, Suite E
North Brunswick, NJ 08902
http://www.bridgelogos.com

To my husband,
John Chatham,
my best friend—whose loving
support has made an invaluable
contribution to the preparation of
Fasting: A Biblical-Historical Study

CONTENTS

FOREWORD

This work is characterized by a careful summary of the biblical and historical basis for the practice of fasting. Extra-biblical as well as biblical sources are utilized in order to examine the methods, motives and theological dimensions of fasting.

After the author defines fasting, she discusses briefly this practice in various religions and cults. However, the heart of this study is an examination of fasting in the Old Testament, Intertestamental Period, New Testament and the Post-Biblical Period, including the present era.

The study is illuminating from a biblical and historical perspective and makes clear that fasting has been part of the religious life of mankind. "Like a scarlet thread woven the length of a linen garment, fasting has endured from ancient history to the present.

French L. Arrington, Ph.D.
Professor of New Testament Greek and Exegesis

PREFACE

A personal interest in fasting has led me to examine its doctrinal basis from a biblical and historical perspective. In this book I define fasting and point out its primary religious significance. I have reviewed each biblical account as it appears in the KJV, and I have researched extra-biblical, intertestamental and post-biblical fasting.

The methods and motives of fasting vary from culture to culture and century to century. However certain themes related to fasting—mourning, repentance, humility, and petition—prevail throughout Scripture and history. These themes reveal the motives for fasting.

Methods for fasting and the time to fast—between Christ's death and return—are clearly defined by integrating both the Old and New Testaments. The length and frequency of either voluntary public or private fasting are an individual matter. Fasting is an intimate act of service or worship between the believer and the Father.

I hope the conclusions I have made in this book will be a means by which the pendulum of fasting swings away from traditional notions of men toward a correct biblical perspective. These thoughts are subject to further scriptural light; however, I believe this study is a much needed step in the right direction.

I have added a chapter of testimonies to inspire and challenge you to the discipline of fasting. It is a record of miracles and wonders that have confirmed the value and effectiveness of fasting. I have noted a few negative possibilities, and provided some practical suggestions in order that you may have an ample guide for your fasting.

I gratefully acknowledge the encouragement of Dr. French Arrington, Reverend F.J. May, and Mr. Henry O'Neal, who read the manuscript. I am especially grateful to Dr. Arrington for writing the foreword. Many thanks go to those several dedicated Christians friends who have taken their precious time to share their testimonies. This manuscript would not be complete without their valuable contribution. The librarians of both Tomlinson College and Lee University are due thanks for patiently assisting in research. I also appreciate all those who were kind enough to respond to the questionnaire.

Romara Dean Chatham

INTRODUCTION

Contemporary authors of books on fasting promise power, strong faith, deliverance and health. In fact, they promise a catalog of spiritual, mental and physical benefits in exchange for days without food. The consciousness may be altered, impossibilities may become possible, nations may be shaped, and battles may be won by fasting. To some writers fasting is a literal cure-all. Are these promises valid? Does the Bible support these statements? What is truth and what is fiction? Is fasting necessary for the twentieth-century Christian or is it a superstition of the past, not applicable today? I will address these and other questions by presenting the biblical and historical records as they exist in order to draw from them a better understanding of the significance and practice of fasting as Scripture intends. I will also examine the testimonies of certain groups and individuals and their fasting experiences.

I must begin this study by defining "fasting," since numerous definitions are given in a variety of dictionaries, encyclopedias and books. Some include absolutely every deviation from the regular habit of eating, calling these partial fasts, abstinences, or explicit fasts. However, to arrive at the original meaning of the word, I will examine the term as derived from the Hebrew, Chaldee and Greek words.

The Hebrew words *tsoom* and *tsome* mean to cover over the mouth, that is, to fast. The Chaldee word *tevawth'* used in Daniel 6:18, means hunger or fasting. The other Hebrew word *'anah*, which explicitly refers to fasting, is used in Leviticus 16:29, 31; 23:27, 32; Numbers 29:7; 30:13 Ezra 8:21; Psalm 35:13; Isaiah 58:3, 5, 10; and Daniel 10:12.[1] The word is translated "afflict oneself" "chasten oneself" or "humble oneself" in the King James Version.

The Greek words used in the New Testament are *nestis, nesteia, nesteuo,* and *asitos. Nestis* is from the negative particle *ne* (not) and *esthio* (eat) meaning abstinence from food for religious reasons.[2] From this nesteuo ("fast") and *nesteia* ("fasting") are derived.[3] *Asitos*, which is used in Acts 27:33, means "without food" or "fasting.[4]

In New Testament times, Jewish custom commanded that "in order to be a proper fast, it must be continued from one sundown till after the next, when the stars appeared and for about twenty-six hours the most rigid abstinence from all food and drink was enjoined."[5] *The Oxford Dictionary of the Christian Church* gives following definition: "In early times fasting entire abstinence from food for the whole or part of the fast day."[6] According to

x

our Lord's words, fasting is having nothing to eat. He said, "They continue with me now three days, and have nothing to eat: and I will not send them away fasting lest they faint" (Matt. 15:32).

Fasting, in one form or another, has been practised since antiquity. In the ancient world it was chiefly done in relation to demons and deities. "The original and most powerful reason for fasting in antiquity," according to Johannes Behm, "is to be found in fear of demons who gained power over men by eating." In the Greek and Roman cultures it was customary to abstain in order to receive ecstatic revelations. In other cultures it was customary to fast following a death because it was believed that there was danger of demonic infection if one ate or drank while the dead person's soul was near. Mystery religionists fasted to prepare for unity with their deity. Fasting was also used in magic and by soothsayers. Some cultures in the ancient Near East used prayer and fasting as a means to have their requests fulfilled by the gods.[7]

Fasting also became customary in every major religion, including Christianity, Judaism, Mohammedism, Buddhism and Hinduism. It is also found in primitive religions from Alaska to Australasia.[8]

Their motives vary. Hindus fast to "raise one's consciousness to union with God." Buddhists fasted to guard, control and lift the senses to a peak experience. Muslims fast each year during the daylight hours of the month of Ramadan to invoke Allah's blessing, to develop spiritual discipline and self-control, to purify the body and spirit, and to evoke in themselves sensitivity and generosity toward the poor. The American Plains indians have learned that fasting causes one to be sensitive to visions and dreams.[9]

Fasting marks important events in the lives of many people. It was part of the initiation rites into the ancient mystery cults of Isis, Attis, and Mithra, and still is among the people of Ojibwa, North America, Brazil, Gran Chaco and several islands of the Pacific. Sioux males and Chiriguano females fast at puberty. The primitive people of East Africa, Guyana, Alaska and Bengal fast before marriage, as do Orthodox Jewish couples. Orthodox Jews and inhabitants of the Andaman Islands, Fiji, Samoa, China, Korea and Africa fast as part of their mourning rituals.[10]

Diverse peoples fast during anticipated danger and in penitence. The females of the Babar Islands fast while the males are at war. While on hunting or whaling expeditions, the Indians of Nootka Sound and Portland Inlet fast. Occasionally Germans fast during severe storms. Ancient Babylonian psalms attest occasions of fasting in penitence or to propitiate gods and spirits. The Zulus have a saying, "The continually stuffed body cannot see secret things." Pythagoras fasted forty days for enlightenment. The Cure of Ars fasted continually and demonstrated remarkable sanctity.[11]

In addition to these examples, fasting has been used for physical, political, and social concens. These fasts are not toward God. The health fasts intended for one's own physical well-being. The political and social fasts are meant to persuade people or governments to respond to a particular problem.

The Greek philosophers Plato and Socrates, who

lived in the fourth and fifth centuries before Christ, "recommended fasting for increasing mental and physical effectiveness." Ancient physicians such as Avicenna, Paracelsus and Hippocrates "advocated fasting for treating a varied range of illnesses." Even today some doctors advise fasting for dieting purposes. Russian physicians report phenomenal success in curing several major illnesses by supervising a fast of thirty days or more for patients.[12]

Mohandas Gandhi "used fasting as a penance and as a means of political protest," believing that one could not pray without fasting or fast without praying. He described his fast as "the prayer of a soul in agony." Dick Gregory fasted to protest America involvement in the Vietnam War. MacSwiney, perhaps the first in history to starve himself to death for a political purpose, has been followed by a number of IRA members who have died in protest fasting.[13]

In 1928 women who had been placed in prison for protesting won by their fasting the right to work and vote. In recent years Cesar Chavez fasted for fair pay for immigrants.[14] The Pentecostal group known as the Siberian Seven fasted to obtain permission to leave Russia.

Has this historical background influenced conscientious twentieth-century Christians to misunderstand biblical fasting? Have books by current authors, especially health advocates, perpetuated a mindset that undermines the power of prayer alone? Has faith been weakened by statements such as "Some battles can only be won through fasting"? If fasting brings power and faith beyond prayer alone, what of those individuals too ill to be won through fasting"? If fasting brings power and faith beyond prayer alone, what of those individuals too ill to fast? What will be the source of their overcoming power?

What does Scripture intend to reveal about fasting? Is it to bring power? Or to discipline the body? Or is it an act of repentance and humility? Or does biblical fasting promise all of these? The act and results of fasting must not be discredited, but it must be tested in the light of the Scriptures. In order to allow the Word of God to speak to us on this subject, we may need to reject some presuppositions which we now hold. I have come to this research with an open mind to the voice of the Word and Spirit to learn what God would have me understand about fasting. To understand fasting by the criterion of the Scriptures is the goal of this book.

In placing the spotlight on fasting it is not my intention to bring it forward as a new doctrine, because it has been practiced from antiquity as I have shown. Further, I will not insist that it be regarded more highly than Scripture teaches, nor will I discredit its rightful place. I will concern myself only with religious fasting, that is, fasting directed toward God. Although certain physical benefits are apparent from fasting, the spiritual benefits will be the main issue. At times, historical evidence will be presented; however, the biblical accounts will be decisive to my conclusions. The historical accounts will appear as nearly as possible in chronological sequence. The biblical fasts will be reviewed book by book as they occur in the testaments.

Chapter 1

The Pentateuch

"Noah found grace in the eyes of the Lord" (Gen. 6:8), Abraham "was called the Friend of God" (James 2:23), the Abrahamic covenant was confirmed to Isaac and Jacob (Gen. 26:3, 4; 28:4), and Joseph was blessed with mercy and favor (Gen. 39:21), yet we have no record of fasting by these patriarchs. The only Genesis account which suggests fasting is that of Abraham's servant who was sent to secure a bride for Isaac. He merely postponed eating until his errand was accomplished (Gen. 24:33). Postponing a meal is not fasting, however.

The story of biblical fasting actually began with Moses atop Mount Sinai. Moses had led the children of Israel from Egypt to the Sinai wilderness. He had already ascended the mount and communed with God twice (Exod. 19:3, 20). The first visit was the occasion of the covenant between God and Israel (Exod. 19:3-9). On the second visit Moses received various ordinances (Exod. 19:20-23:33). Then the Lord called Moses to the top of the mount a third time (Exod. 24). Nadab, Abihu, and seventy of the elders were allowed to witness God's glory somewhere below the pinnacle of the mount and there they ate and drank. Then God called Moses higher up the mountain to receive the two tablets of the covenant with the law and commandments written on them. The plans for the tabernacle and its ministry were also revealed to the Israelite leader. As Moses recounted this glorious event before Israel's second generation almost forty years later, he told them that he had been on the mount forty days and nights without bread or water (Deut. 9:9).

When Moses was ready to take the tablets of Testimony down the mount, God told him that the people had molded a calf and were worshiping it (Exod 32:7-35). God threatened to destroy them, but their leader pleaded for mercy and they were spared. As Moses descended the mountain and saw the naked Israelites dancing around the golden calf, he cast the tables of stone upon the ground, breaking them. After the destruction of the calf Moses returned to the top of the mountain (Exod. 34:4-28).

He stayed on Sinai another forty days and nights without food or water (Exod. 34:28; Deut. 9:18; 10:10). Moses' specific purpose for fasting this time was to avert God's wrath over the sins of Aaron and the people. The Lord was so angry with them that He threatened to destroy them. God heard Moses' prayer and spared their lives (Deut. 9:18-20).

The biblical record indicates at least two days between the two fasts and perhaps longer. However, it does not indicate whether Moses ate between the two fasts. Due to the distressing nature of the situation, it is possible that Moses did not eat for the entire period. If that is true, this is the longest recorded biblical fast. Of course, Moses must have been supernaturally sustained because no one can live more than a few days without water.

The only other fast mentioned in the Pentateuch is that of the Day of Atonement (Lev. 16:29-34; 23:27-32; Num. 29:7-11). Otherwise, the only mention of fasting is that a woman is permitted to fast if her husband allows her (Num. 30:13).

The phrase used for fasting on the Day of Atonement is "afflict the soul." The context of the law given concerning the Day of Atonement is the death of Aaron's sons, Nadab and Abihu, who were not properly sanctified to offer a sacrifice before the Lord and who offered fire which God had not commanded (Lev. 10:1-3). Immediately following careful instructions regarding the preparation of the high priest for offering sacrifices and the offering of those sacrifices, the perpetual statute concerning the observance of the Day of Atonement is given (Lev. 16).

On this day the Israelites were to abstain from food and work. Food could not be prepared or consumed by anyone of their own nation or even strangers that dwelt among them (Lev. 16:29). Anyone who did not fast was to be excommunicated. The day was a sabbath of rest on which a public meeting was held and burnt offerings and confession for the sins of the past year were made unto the Lord. Each year on this day the high priest took the blood of the sin-offering into the Holy of Holies and sprinkled it on the mercy seat. If anyone worked on this day he was to be punished by death.

The celebration began in the evening of the ninth day of the seventh month and continued until the evening of the tenth day of the month (Lev. 23:26- 32). The fast was observed for twenty-four to twenty-six hours, "from before sundown, when it is still light outside, until after the next sundown, when it is dark outside and three stars can be seen in the sky."[1]

This day preceded the Feast of the Tabernacles by about five days. The Feast of the Tabernacles celebrates the completion of the fall harvest of grapes and olives. This event, in sharp contrast with the Day of Atonement, was a joyous feast. In fact, of the five special days (Passover, Pentecost, Trumpets, Tabernacles and the Day of Atonement) which the Lord commanded Israel to observe, all but the last were feast days.

Originally, God instructed only the high priest to wear special clothing for the Day of Atonement. He was to wear a white linen garment into the Holy of Holies, his regal ceremonial robes laid aside.[2] Eventually, the rabbis also imposed restrictions on the people. "According to the Mishna, Yoma 8:1, on the Day of Atonement it is forbidden to eat, or drink, or bathe, anoint oneself, or wear sandals, or to indulge in conjugal intercourse."[3] Sackcloth was normally worn in the Ancient Near East to symbolize grief (Gen. 37:34) and penitence II Chron. 21:16). Ashes sprinkled upon the head also were a sign of grief (Josh. 7:6). The association of sackcloth and ashes with fasting gradually became a Jewish tradition.

Alfred Edersheim wrote the following about late public fasts:

> The practice was to bring the ark which contained the rolls of the law from the synagogue into the streets, and to strew ashes

upon it. The people all appeared covered
with sackcloth and ashes. Ashes were
publicly strewn on the heads of the elders
and judges. Then one more venerable than
the rest would address the people, his sermon
being based on such admonition as this: "My
brethren, it is not said of the men of Nineveh,
that God had respect to their sackcloth or
their fasting, but that 'God saw their works,
that they turned from their evil way.'
Similarly, it is written in the 'traditions' (of
the prophets): 'Rend your heart, and not your
garments and turn unto Jehovah your God.'
". . . Confession of sin and prayer mingled
with the penetential Psalms. In Jerusalem they
gathered at the eastern gate, and seven times
as the voice of prayer ceased, they bade the
priests 'blow!' . . . After prayer, the people
retired to the cemeteries to mourn and weep.[4]

Abraham Z. Idelsohn says that "many pious Jews used
to remain in the Synagogue twenty-four hours standing on
their feet, reading and praying without interruption."[5]

In addition to the Day of Atonement, or *Yom Kippur,*
the Jews were later required to fast from sundown to
sundown for *Tish'ah BeAv* which commemorated the
destruction of the first and second temples. All other Jewish
fasts were "observed from day-break to nightfall only" by
abstaining from food and water.[6] Generally speaking during
biblical times Hebrews ate only two meals each day, one
between about nine in the morning and noon and the other
in the evening.[7] Whether the fast was the twenty-four to
twenty-six hour fast of the Day of Atonement or *Tish'ah
BeAv* or one of the other daybreak-to-night fall fasts,

probably only the morning meal was missed. This was true of the valiant men of Jabesh-gilead's seven-day mourning fast for Saul, and David's mourning fasts for Saul and Abner (1 Sam. 31:1and 2 Sam. 1:12, 3:35). They apparently ate each day after the sun went down.

The law for fasting on the annual Day of Atonement was explicitly made a perpetual ordinance; however, Paul wrote in the New Testament period that the Old Testament ordinances were blotted out, taken out of the way and nailed to the cross with Christ (Col. 2:14). Therefore, we are no longer required to fast on the Day of Atonement. It did continue to be observed by devout Jews throughout New Testament times (Acts 27:9) and to this present day is obligatory in Reform Judaism.

It is important to notice that the only other fast which God ordained in the entire Old Testament was when He called His people to a repentant fast through the prophet Joel (Joel 2:12-18). This infrequency of a required fast and the relationship of fasting with repentance is significant. All other public and private fasts recorded in the Old Testament were self-imposed.

CHAPTER 2

THE HISTORICAL BOOKS

Joshua

During the conquest of the promised land, Joshua sent men to Ai to spy the land. The men reported to Joshua that only two or three thousand men were needed to conquer the area because it was small. About three thousand men were sent, but they were chased from the town and lost thirty-six men in the battle. Joshua was so distressed that he and the elders rent their clothes, sprinkled ashes on their heads and remained prostrate before the Ark of the Covenant until the evening (Josh. 7:6). It is uncertain whether fasting accompanied this act of distress, but it is possible. However, the Lord told him to get up off his face, for Israel had sinned. As soon as Achan confessed his breach of the covenant in taking the spoil from Ai, and once Achan, his family, their personal effects, and the spoil were destroyed, God gave Israel the battle.

Judges

As a Levite traveled with his concubine from Bethelehem-judah toward Mount Ephraim they found lodging with an old man in Gibeath. After dinner lewd men of the city came to the house and tried to force the old man to relinquish the Levite to them so they could commit homosexual acts with him. The old man refused but offered his own daughter and the Levite's concubine to them, but the men would not have them. Then the Levite himself brought his concubine to them. The scoundrels raped her and abused her all night. About daybreak the woman came back to the old man's house and died on the threshold. When the Levite went out of the house the next morning he found her dead. He then reported the rape and murder to each of the tribes of Israel.

The leaders of all the tribes held an assembly to decide what action they would take. They first asked for the Gibeathites who had committed the crime, but the Benjamites of whose tribe they belonged would not deliver them to the men of Israel. Instead, the Benjamites prepared for war. The children of Israel went to the house of the Lord to inquire of Him which tribe should go to battle first. Judah was chosen and that day twenty-two thousand of them were killed.

Again the Israelites prepared for battle and the people went to the house of God weeping and asking God's counsel until evening. The Lord instructed them to fight against the Benjamites again. On the second day eighteen thousand Israelites were killed. Then all the people of Israel went to the Lord's house where they wept, fasted, offered burnt offerings and peace offerings, and sat before the Lord until evening. Upon enquiring of the Lord's will, the reply was, "Go up; for to morrow I will deliver them into thine hand" (Judg. 20:28). On the third day Israel won the battle with ease, slaying all but six hundred Benjamites who fled to the wilderness.[1]

The significance of fasting in this civil war account is difficult to determine. It is true that on the day following the fast the Lord gave them the battle. However, Israel had gone to the house of the Lord to learn His will concerning the battle all three days. Further, the last two days they had wept before the Lord until evening waiting for His guidance. On the third day fasting and sacrifices were added to the worship. The sacrifices were burnt offerings and peace offerings. The burnt offering was offered voluntarily and was for atonement (Lev.1:4). The peace offerings symbolized a right relationship with God and could also symbolize thanksgiving.[2] The fasting and sacrifices offered in the public meeting until evening resemble the prescribed ceremony of the Day of Atonement. Even the sitting before the Lord recalls the sabbath of rest ordained for that special day of reconciliation with God. In this act of fasting and sacrificing the people were expressing to God their earnest desire to be in a right relationship with Him. God responded to that attitude by giving them the victory in battle.

1 Samuel

The books of 1 and 2 Samuel, 1 and 2 Kings, and 1 and 2 Chronicles cover the activity of the last of the judges, but especially from the rule of the kings to the Babylonian captivity. The events of 2 Samuel and 1 and 2 Kings are repeated in 1 and 2 Chronicles.

During Eli's judgeship, Hannah was so distressed because of her barrenness and the provocation of her husband's other fruitful wife that she wept and didn't eat (I Sam. 1:7). She is one of several in the Scriptures whose souls were in such anguish they could not eat. These are not considered religious fasts.

While Samuel was judge, Israel was being oppressed by the Philistines. At the same time God's people were worshiping their Canaanite neighbors' fertility gods, Baal and Ashtaroth. The worship ritual of these gods involved sexual rites, which were an affront to God's holiness. Further, they had broken the first commandment, "Thou shalt have no other gods before me." Samuel admonished all Israel to return to God and serve Him only. The judge asked for a public meeting of all Israel.

During this assembly Samuel prayed for them and offered a burnt offering to the Lord. The people drew water and poured it out before the Lord and fasted that day. Pouring out the water symbolized confession and humiliation before God.[3] As the sacrifice was being offered the Philistines approached to attack. Samuel cried to the Lord for help, and Israel defeated their enemy so badly that the Philistines never attempted another invasion as long as Samuel lived. In commemoration of the victory, Samuel set up a memorial stone at the site of battle and named the place "Ebenezer" or "stone of help."

The public gathering and its accompanying penitent acts are very similar to those of the Day of Atonement and the account in Judges which we have noted. In Judges and here in 1 Samuel 7, when Israel came before God united with contrite hearts symbolized by overt acts of praying, fasting, sacrificing, and in this case, pouring out water before the Lord, God responded to their need.

The remaining fasting narratives in 1 Samuel are nonreligious. It is unfortunate that the only fasts recorded of King Saul were not directed or approved by God. As Saul and six hundred men were pursued by three companies of Philistines, the king made an oath that none of them would eat until evening (1 Sam. 14:24). If anyone broke the fast, he would be punished by death. Saul's rash vow almost cost him the life of his son, who was unaware of the vow and innocently ate some honey.

In addition, the other men became so weak from hunger that they killed the spoil of the battle, that is, the sheep, oxen, and calves, and ate them with the blood, which was strictly forbidden in the law (Lev. 17:10-16). It is interesting that in other battles, which were preceded by proper fasting, the people were strengthened to fight so that they did not faint. In contrast, the result of this fast was disastrous.

On another occasion, at dinner one evening Saul became enraged with Jonathan for protecting David (1 Sam. 20). The king attempted to kill Jonathan with his javelin. Jonathan was so angry he left the table without eating.

Subsequent to this, the Philistines once again prepared for battle against Israel. Saul, upon seeing the host, became terrified. He inquired of the Lord and received no reply by dream, by Urim, or by the prophets. He was so desperate that he went against his own ban against witches and visited the witch of Endor so that she might summon Samuel from the dead. When Samuel informed Saul that the next day

Israel would be taken by the Philistines and that he and his sons would die, Saul fell to the ground in fear and weakness. In his distress he had not eaten for a day and night (1 Sam. 28). This was Saul's final fast, for the next day he and his sons died in battle. In fact, after Saul was badly wounded he purposely fell upon his own sword. Disgracefully, his body was stripped, beheaded and fastened to the wall of Bethshan by the Philistines (1 Sam. 31).

During this same battle some of David's warriors found an unconscious Egyptian servant who had fallen ill and been left in a field by his master. He had been without food or water for three days until David's troops fed him (1 Sam. 30:11-13).

The final fast in the book of 1 Samuel was a mourning fast by the valiant men of Jabesh-gilead. Saul had delivered Jabesh-gilead from the Ammonites (1 Sam. 11), and now they honored him in his death. They rescued the bodies of Saul and his two sons from the wall of Bethshan, buried them, and mourned for seven days. This extended fast did not include nights. It was probably from sunrise to sunset each day so that one meal was taken after sunset every day (1 Sam. 31:13; 1 Chron. 10:12).

2 Samuel

This second section of Samuel opens with a one-day mourning fast for Saul and his sons. David and his men rent their clothes, mourned, wept, and fasted until evening (2 Sam. 1:11-12). These were the customary expressions of mourning.

David later led a mourning fast at the death of Abner, captain of Saul's army (2 Sam. 3:31-35). This also was a fast until sunset. Both these men, Saul and Abner, were enemies to David. Saul had tried to kill David and Abner had revolted against him. Yet at their death David honored them in mourning.

After Bathsheba was with child by David, he sent to the battlefield for her husband, Uriah (2 Sam. 11). David's intention was that Uriah spend some time with his wife so Uriah would appear to be the father of the child. However, the soldier said he could not abide in his house or eat or drink while the ark and God's people were living in tents. Eventually, David got him drunk, but Uriah never went to his house or ate. This fast apparently was a fast of sympathy and camaraderie rather than one with spiritual intention.

The only fast of spiritual significance in 2 Samuel was observed by David (12:15-23). The prophet Nathan confronted the king for his adultery with Bathsheba. David confessed his sin. Nathan said that the Lord had blotted out his sin but that the child would die. As Nathan had prophesied, the child became ill. In sackcloth David sought the Lord, laying upon the ground and fasting. Although the elders or Sheikhs of his family, who normally had considerable influence upon the king, urged him to eat, he would not.

On the seventh day the child died and David's servants despaired to tell him of the death lest he would do more harm to himself. But when David realized the child was dead, he arose from the earth, washed, and anointed himself, changed his clothes and went to the house of the Lord to worship. Afterward, to the astonishment of his servants, David ate. They expected him to fast after the child's death, according to custom. The king responded that he had fasted and wept while the child was alive, hoping that God would be merciful and allow the child to live.

This is the first recorded personal penitent fast. David had confessed his sin before the child's illness began. Fasting, sackcloth and lying on the ground added impetus to his confession. The child was dying because of David's sin. David hoped that God, seeing the depth of David's remorse, would allow the child to live. But his fasting and repentance did not change the mind of God. Sin had to be punished.

1 Kings

Three occasions of fasting during the period of the divided kingdom are contained within the book of 1 Kings. In chapter 13 an unnamed man of God from Judah was sent on a prophetic mission to Bethel to foretell the destruction of the idolatrous altar of the northern kingdom. Besides giving him a message to carry to Bethel, the Lord instructed him not to eat or drink while there and to return to Judah by a different route. To eat and drink with them would have signified entrance into covenant relations with a rebellious people.[4]

King Jeroboam tried to entice him to eat, but he refused the delicacies of the king's table in obedience to the Lord's command. However, as the prophet returned home, a false prophet deceived him by saying that an angel of the Lord had told him that the prophet was now permitted to eat and drink. After following these erroneous instructions, the man of God died a sudden, tragic death at the paw of a lion. Upon hearing news of his death, the lying prophet confessed, "It is the man of God, who was disobedient unto the word of the Lord: therefore the Lord hath delivered him unto the lion" (1 Kings 13:26).

This fast was not directed toward God, but was in direct obedience to God. Its purpose was to refrain from entering into an alliance and identifying with an idolatrous nation.

Chapter 19 tells of Elijah's fast of forty days and nights as he journeyed from Beersheba of Judah to Mount Horiba (Sinai). He walked the distance of about 480 kilometers, or 12 kilometers daily (1 Kings 19:8).[5] On Mount Horeb the Lord encouraged Elijah. Prior to this visitation, the man of God was despondent because he thought Jezebel had slain all of the prophets of God except himself; and she had threatened to kill him. He despaired for his life and asked the Lord to let him die. Following his mountaintop experience with God, he resumed his ministry with fervor, without recurring depression. He was energized with boldness and zest to accomplish the prophetic tasks.

Elijah's fast without food or drink recalls Moses' supernatural fast on the same mountain. Moses represents the law; Elijah represents the prophets. Subsequent to Elijah's fast, an angel prepared a cake and water for him which sustained him for forty days and nights.

Fasting occurs three times in chapter 21 regarding the same incident. Near the palace of Ahab, king of the northern kingdom, was a vineyard which belonged to Naboth, a Jezreelite. The king offered to purchase it for a fair price or trade it for a better one, but Naboth would not sell his piece of ground, because it had been handed down to him by his fathers. An inheritance was sacred to him as a Jew and he was responsible to pass it to his posterity.[6]

Ahab became so angry he wouldn't eat. His wife, Jezebel, proclaimed a fast using the king's signature. The fast indicated that someone had offended God and the offender had to be purged or calamity would come upon the entire community.[7] She instructed the elders and nobles of Naboth's city to have a trial in which two sons of Belial would accuse him of blaspheming God and the king. The scheme was carried out and Naboth was stoned to death for his alleged crime.

The scheme was condemned by Elijah, who pronounced doom on Ahab and his family, whereupon Ahab humbled himself by rending his clothes, wearing sackcloth, fasting, lying in sackcloth and going softly before the Lord. God recognized Ahab's going softly before the Lord. God recognized Ahab's humiliation and postponed judgment until his son's reign.

2 Chronicle

When King Jehoshaphat of Judah received news of the approaching allied forces of the Moabites, Ammonites, and Edomites, he proclaimed a national fast to seek the Lord. The people with their families from all the cities of the southern kingdom gathered together in the house of the Lord to fast and pray. The invading host outnumbered Judah and victory was, naturally speaking, hopeless, but the Lord gave His Word. Early the next morning the Israelites began marching toward the wilderness of Tekoa led by singers who were praising the Lord. As they worshiped the Lord, He fought the battle for them. Additionally, He delivered to them such an abundant spoil of riches that it took three days to gather. Their seeking the Lord with prayers and fasting was remarkably rewarded (2 Chron. 20).

This account makes no mention of repentance or humbling themselves, only that the people gathered in the temple fasting, praying, and standing before the Lord seeking Him for help. It was said of Jehoshaphat that he had prepared his heart to seek God before this urgent crisis arose (2 Chron. 19). This was a petitionary fast.

Ezra

The books of Ezra, Nehemiah and Esther span about the last one hundred years of Old Testament history. Ezra and Nehemiah were involved with the events of the returning Jews from Babylonian captivity. Ezra was in charge of an expedition of seventeen hundred Jews who were returning to their homeland carrying rich treasures for the Temple. This was a trip of approximately nine hundred miles, which took about four months.[8]

Ezra was a devout priest and scribe who sought, practiced and taught the law of the Lord (Ezra 7:10). He had witnessed to Artaxerxes, king of Babylon, that the hand of God was upon all those who seek Him (Ezra 8:22). Now Ezra was faced with the extended journey to Jerusalem. He knew there was inevitably a possibility of an ambush by bandits along the road, hut, because of his testimony before the king, he was ashamed to ask for protection on the journey. So the priest proclaimed a fast to seek of God a safe journey for the caravan and its precious cargo.

Notice the conditions. Ezra was on a mission for God. His heart was right with God. He wanted God to receive the glory and he had confidence in God for protection. Added to these conditions were fasting and seeking God. Needless to say, they were protected for the duration of the journey (Ezra 8). This may be considered a petitionary fast similar to Jehoshaphat's.

After the expedition arrived in Jerusalem, the local leaders brought disturbing news to Ezra. The Jewish people, including the clergy, had married non-Jewish women, which was forbidden by God's law (Deut. 7:1-5). These wives had brought with them their idol worship, which was considered to have been a major factor in the nation's downfall under the kings.[9] In addition to the idolatry, intermarriage would have led to the extinction of the Jewish nation.

Ezra was so stunned that he immediately rent his garment and mantle and plucked off the hair of his head and beard. At the evening sacrifice (3 P.M.) he fell to his knees before the congregation and, spreading his hands before God, wept, prayed and confessed the sins of the people. He prayed in the first person plural, sharing the responsibility of their transgressions, although his own heart and life were right with God. The crowd was moved to tears of repentance and plans were made to systematically make restitution in putting away the alien wives. Ezra continued his remorse in the chamber of Johanan, the high priest, where he neither ate nor drank because of the sins of Israel (Ezra 10:6). This may have been a time when Ezra could not eat because of his grief over this matter or it may have been a repentant fast.

Nehemiah

Nehemiah was one of those Jews who had settled in Persia and did not plan to return to Judah. He was the king's cupbearer, a position just behind the crown prince in the king's attendance. He was probably a eunuch, whose job was to taste the king's wine to determine whether it was poison.[10]

One of his brothers, Hanani, and some other Jews returned from a visit in Judah. Nehemiah inquired about the affairs of the Jews who had been left behind during the exile and about the Holy City. He was told that the remnant was in great affliction and reproach and the walls and gates of the city lay destroyed. A city was no city without walls. When Nehemiah heard this distressing news, he sat down, wept, mourned, fasted and prayed over the plight of his kinsmen. As he prayed, he confessed the sins of Israel and asked for God's mercy (Neh. 1).

More than three months passed, and Artaxerxes noticed the sad countenance of his servant. The cupbearer was afraid. The monarch had recently commissioned Rehum and Shimshai to stop the rebuilding and refortification of Jerusalem (Ezra 4:17-24). After prayer, Nehemiah requested permission to rebuild Jerusalem's walls. He further asked for a military escort, and timber with which to rebuild the gates and walls. The Persian king granted his requests (Neh. 2).

Nehemiah maintained a constant relationship with God. He was a praying man (2:4; 4:4, 5; 5:19; 6:14; 13:14, 22, 29, 31).[11] His concern was for the condition of the Jews. Repentance and petition are evident in this fast.

Nehemiah also recorded a general fast on the twenty-fourth day of the seventh month (Neh. 9, 10). For over three weeks the children of Israel had gathered each day in the streets to hear the Torah read and explained. They had discovered and observed the Feast of Tabernacles. On the eighth day of the feast they had kept the solemn assembly in which no work was done but when sacrifices were made (Num. 29:35-40).

Although the Day of Atonement was not kept, the people assembled and fasted with sackcloth and ashes. They separated themselves from all strangers and confessed their sins and those of their fathers. One-fourth of the day was spent reading the law and another fourth spent confessing sins and worshiping God. Then they renewed their covenant in writing to keep the ancient law of God as given to Moses.

On this day, as on the Day of Atonement, fasting was related to reconciliation with God. No sacrifices were made and the high priest did not enter the Holy of Holies, but at least half the day was spent repenting, worshiping God, and renewing their covenant.

Esther

Between the seventh and twelfth year of the rule of King Ahasuerus (Xerxes), Mordecai refused to bow before and reverence Haman (who was second to the king) as the king commanded. In recompense, Haman determined to have all the Jews destroyed in eleven months. Upon receiving the proclamation, the Jews in every providence began fasting, mourning, weeping, wailing, and laying in sackcloth and ashes (Esther 4:3). Mordecai asked his cousin, Queen Esther, whom he had reared, to request that the order be annulled by the king. Esther hesitated because there was a law that if anyone approached the king's court unbidden, he would be put to death unless the king admitted him with a golden sceptre (Esther 4:11).

Esther determined to request audience with the king, but not before she proclaimed a fast among the Jews of Shushan, the city of the royal palace. She asked that they fast with her and her maidens for three days and nights without food or water.

On the third day the queen dressed in her royal apparel and waited in the inner court of the palace (Esther 5:1). When the king saw her standing in the court, he extended the golden sceptre toward her. Ultimately, Haman was hanged upon the gallows he had prepared for Mordecai. Mordecai was promoted to Haman's position and the Jews were spared.

The Jews' spontaneous fast upon receiving the proclamation of their impending destruction was one of mourning. The fast proclaimed by Esther was for her protection and aid (Esther 4.16); clearly, it was not a fast of mourning or of pentitence, but of petition.

CHAPTER 3

THE POETICAL AND WISDOM BOOKS

Job

The only hint of fasting in the book of Job is when Elihu reasoned with Job that God chastens man with pain so that he is too ill to eat and until he becomes so thin his bones protrude. This cannot be considered a religious fast, but rather a loss of appetite due to the painful condition of the individual.

Psalms

David, true to his character, fasted for his false accusers during their illness (Ps. 35:11-15). He donned sackcloth and fasted and prayed for them as though they were his friends or brothers. He bowed himself heavily as one who mourned for his own mother.

This fast was apparently one of mourning and petition.[1] That David humbled his soul with fasting recalls the words of the Lord when Ahab fasted, and the meaning of *Yom Kippur,* which is "to afflict oneself." Therefore, David's fast was also an act of humiliation.

In Psalm 69 David cried out to God for deliverance from the murky floodwaters which were about to engulf him. Those who hated him were more numerous than the hairs of his head. When he wept with fasting it was to his reproach. When he wore the sackcloth of mourning he was a byword to his enemies.

David's motive for fasting in this passage is unclear. Apparently, it was a mourning or pentitential fast, because of the association with sackcloth. Verse 10 says, "When I wept, and chastened my soul with fasting, that was to my reproach." The words "and chastened" were not in the original text.

In Psalm 102:4 the psalmist was in such trouble he forgot to eat. This refers to a loss of appetite and not a fast for spiritual reasons.

Another time David complained of his enemies and asked God to punish them. He asked for mercy for himself because he was poor and needy. His heart was wounded within him and his knees were weak and his body was gaunt from fasting (Ps. 109:24). He did not hint at his motive for this extended fast which had caused his weakness and weight loss.

From these remarks by David, along with fasting stories in 2 Samuel, we can safely assume that David was well acquainted with fasting. He repented, he mourned and he humbled himself in fastings.

CHAPTER 4

THE BOOKS OF THE MAJOR PROPHETS

Isaiah

Apparently the custom of fasting continued throughout the period of the major prophets. The entire fifty-eighth chapter of the book of Isaiah is given to the subject of fasting. It is the most thorough piece of biblical literature dealing with the matter. In view of the repetitious backsliding that marked the history of the chosen people of God, it is not surprising that this chapter opens with such alarming language as "Cry aloud, spare not, lift up thy voice like a trumpet, and shew my people their transgression, and the house of Jacob their sins" (Isa. 58:1).

God was tired of the Israelites' pretense of worship. They were going through the motions of seeking Him daily and desiring to know the ways by which He would deliver and lead them. They were acting as though they were living righteously and keeping God's holy ordinances. They asked God for "righteous manifestations of judgment," meaning that which would save them and destroy their foes.[1] They delighted in approaching God, because they expected Him to reward their fasts. But He did not respond as they thought He should. When He finally did respond, it was a solemn declaration. God was displeased with them for seeking Him and afflicting themselves without genuine repentance.

Their fast days were not sabbaths of rest but business as usual. They were oppressing their laborers; they were fighting and quarrelling. God would never hear their prayers as long as they continued living in that way. But they afflicted their souls, bowed down their heads like bulrushes, and spread sackcloth and ashes under them. They went through a ritual of a fast, but God would not accept their abstinence because of their merciless treatment of their fellow man.

The fast which God accepts is accompanied by due consideration for one's fellow man. Fasting must include loosing the bonds of wickedness which place men under bondage; freeing the oppressed; breaking bread with the hungry; bringing care to the poor; sheltering the homeless; clothing the naked; and providing help and respect for one's kinsmen.

God promised the Israelites light and health if they would respond satisfactorily toward others. Light is associated with God's love, in contrast with His wrath. Health describes a man near death who is restored to good health. He promised that their righteousness would go before them and that the glory of the Lord would be their rear guard. Frantz Delitzsch noted that:

> When Israel is diligent in the performance
> of works of compassionate love, it is like an

army on the march or a travelling caravan, for which righteousness clears and shows the way as being the most appropriate gift of God, and whose rear is closed by the glory of God, which so conducts it to its goal that not one is left behind.[2]

Finally, God promises to hear every call for help.

The prophet reminded them again that these heavenly blessings are conditional. They had to put away the yoke of oppression. They had to quit pointing a scornful finger at humble and godly men. They had to quit speaking injurious words against their neighbors. They had to distribute alms to the needy and satisfy the needs of those bowed down with abstinence. Only after these gracious considerations would God provide light in the darkness. He would safely and continually guide them. He would satisfy them in times of extreme drought. Their bones would be refreshed and made strong. They would be both productive and supplied with a reservoir, which would not fail. Their offspring would rebuild the ruins and foundations of former times. They would be called by the honorable titles "repairer of the breach" and "restorer of paths."

At the last they were enjoined to keep the Sabbath. Delitzsch believes that the sabbath was prescribed to stop their mundane business from keeping their minds on earthly affairs, so that they might "occupy their minds with God and His word."[3] If they delighted in the sabbath because they could concentrate on God wholly, and did not consider the injunction against taking care of their own affairs a burden, God would reward them with the inheritance promised them.

The point of this entire chapter is that what God desires is not the externals of fasting, but a complete change of heart and life. When the heart and life are right, God responds from heaven. When the heart and life are not right, no matter how much fasting or any other external pretense of worship, the windows of heaven are closed.

Verse 3 mentions that on their fast days they continued to go about their usual business. Verse 13 reminded them of their obligation to keep the sabbath. Such preoccupation with the cares of this life conflicts with the instruction for the Day of Atonement when all work was to cease. A nonfaster was liable to excommunication, but one who worked was liable to punishment by death (Lev. 23:26-32). It seems that God expected their undivided attention on that day. One of the indictments in this chapter against Israel was that they continued their personal pursuits on their fast days.

In verse 4 their motive for fasting was to make God hear them, but He promised to hear their cries only if their living was right. Abstaining from eating, bowing their heads, and sitting in sackcloth and ashes did not in itself bring answers to prayers. God responds spontaneously to those who treat others with love.

Jeremiah

Jeremiah prophesied during the last forty years prior to the fall of Jerusalem. Judah had broken her covenant with God and was involved in idolatry. Jeremiah prophesied a severe drought as a consequence for these sins (14: 1-12). The prophet confessed the iniquity of the people and asked for God's help, but it was too late. God instructed Jeremiah to stop praying for them. Judgment would be visited upon them. Because of their unfaithfulness, God would not accept their fasting and sacrifices. Ritualism is no substitute for true repentance.

Jeremiah 36:6 probably attests the observance of the Day of Atonement. Verse 9 marks a public fast proclaimed in the ninth month of the fifth year of the rule of Jehoiakim, king of Judah. Everyone in the entire province was to observe this fast before the Lord, but it probably was not kept.

Daniel

The book of Daniel describes three occasions of fasting. The first is not a religious fast, but one of anxiety by King Darius over Daniel's plight in the lion's den (Dan. 6:6-23).

In the first year of Darius' rule Daniel realized, after reading Jeremiah's prophecy of Israel's seventy years of bondage, that the captivity was almost ended. So he set his face unto the Lord to seek Him by prayer and supplications, with fasting, sackcloth and ashes (Dan. 9:3). During this time of prayer, fasting and mourning, he confessed the sins of Israel and asked for God's mercy. Although he was a man of God, Daniel spoke in the first person plural, sharing the guilt of all the people. While he was still praying, Gabriel appeared and informed him concerning future events (Dan. 9). Daniel's fast was for the reconciliation of Israel with God. He was not seeking revelation, but forgiveness and mercy.

In the third year of the rule of Cyrus, Daniel fasted the first three weeks of the first month, Nisan (Dan. 10:3). The reference to "bread" in this verse is understood to mean food generally. In other words, he ate no food for the

CHAPTER 5

THE BOOKS OF THE MINOR PROPHETS

Joel

The only other fast, which was ordained by God, besides the Day of Atonement fast, is recorded by Joel. The poet-orator addressed Israel concerning the devastating plague of locusts which had stripped their land bare of vegetation. He asked the elderly men whether they or their fathers had ever witnessed anything like it. This disaster was unparalleled. One swarm after another had invaded the area like a hostile army bent upon destruction until they had "consumed herbage, fruit, leaves of trees . . . young shoots and . . . bark." What the locusts had not devoured, fire and drought had destroyed. The dire circumstances caused a famine for the people and their beasts. The meat and drink offerings had stopped because the corn, new wine, and oil used in these sacrifices were gone. The suspension of the daily sacrifice was the greatest calamity that could fall on Israel, for this meant for the Jew that the covenant relation was suspended.[1]

This occasion is compared with the deepest sorrow of all, that of a virgin whose promised bridegroom has died before the marriage. So Joel called for the priests to gird themselves in sackcloth and lie in it all night mourning and howling (1:13). Only in the worst calamity was sackcloth kept on day and night. The priests were to call an assembly of the elders and all the inhabitants the Temple to fast and cry unto the Lord (1:14). Attendance was to be so stringent that the elders, children, unweaned babies, brides, and bridegrooms were required to participate. Newlyweds were generally exempt from fasting or mourning during the wedding week.[2]

Joel summoned them to return to the Lord with all their heart, with fasting, weeping, and mourning (Joel 2:12). They were to rend their hearts instead of their garments. God wanted a contrite and broken heart rather than mere outward signs of grief. If they genuinely responded to Joel's plea, the Lord would have mercy upon them and answer their cries. He would restore their lands so that there would be plenty.

This was a day of mourning the horrible plague of locusts, and it was a day of repentance. This fast was observed congregated in unity in the temple as on the Day of Atonement. Work subsided until the fast was completed and no sacrifices were made because of the unusual circumstances. Otherwise, this fast resembles the Great Fast of the Law. Again, fasting and repentance are coupled in appealing for reconciliation with God.

Jonah

God sent Jonah to warn the Ninevites about their impending doom, because their wickedness had drawn the attention of God (Jon. 1:1, 2). After Jonah's initial disobedience and rendezvous with the whale, God reiterated the commission (chapter 3). The only message he preached to the city was "Yet forty days, and Nineveh shall be overthrown" (Jon. 3:4). "Overthrown" is the same verb used referring to the destruction of Sodom and Comorrah.[3] Something about the man and his message immediately struck the hearts of the people. Everyone from the nobles to the beggars believed God and fasted in sackcloth and ashes.

When the king received the word he removed his majestic robes and donned sackcloth. Then he stepped from his royal throne and sat in ashes. His public announcement was made throughout the city that neither man nor beast was to eat or drink water. The urgency of the situation would be impressed upon the populace by the constant lowing of the hungry cattle. The king asked that everyone turn from his wickedness and violence, which to the Hebrew meant repentance, implying a complete change of life. God saw their works, not their words, and did not destroy the city.[4]

Jonah's single account of fasting is unique in the Old Testament. Nineveh was a gentile city steeped in idolatry and especially known for their battle atrocities. Jonah did not want to see them spared because they were enemies of Israel. Although we have no record of Jonah telling them to repent or how to repent, they knew what to do and how to do it. Although they were pagans, and did not have the blessing of a prophetic ministry as Israel had, they understood right from wrong. Their forms of penitence are exactly the same as those of Israel. They repented with fasting, while using the common outward penitential symbols of sackcloth and ashes.

33

Zechariah

In the fourth year of Darius, a delegation led by Sherezer and Regemmelech, perhaps from Bethel, came to Jerusalem to pray before the Lord and to enquire whether they should continue observing the fast of the fifth month as they had for so many years (Zech. 7). At this time the new temple was about half finished. The embassy wondered if it was appropriate to continue commemorating the destruction of Jerusalem and the former temple (586 B.C.) with a fast, as they had been doing for about the past seventy years. Other commemorative fasts had also been appointed by their leaders.

In the seventh month the murder of Gedaliah was remembered with a fast day. In the fourth month the conquest of Jerusalem by Nebuchadnezzar was commemorated and in the tenth month the beginning of the siege of Jerusalem by Nebuchadnezzar was commemorated.[5]

Prior to the exile all the annual religious events except the Day of Atonement had been joyous celebrations. John Watts notes, "The exile changed that, putting a veil of sorrow and weeping on the whole of religious life. Laments (of the book of Lamentations) replaced hymns and thanksgiving."[6] The calamities behind the fasts had been brought upon Israel for their lack of keeping the moral precepts which the prophets had constantly preached.[7]

The Lord was not impressed with their self- imposed commemorative fast days, for they were not unto Him. What He required was keeping the words of the former prophets. They were to administer justice in their courts and show mercy and love toward one another. They were not to oppress the widow, orphan, stranger or poor; or devise evil against their neighbors.

The Lord promised them that there would be a time when their fast days would be turned into joy and gladness and cheerful feasts (Zech. 8:19). Zechariah prophetically exhorted them to rejoice greatly because their King was coming (Zech. 9:9).

CHAPTER 6

THE INTERTESTAMENTAL PERIOD

To understand the attitudes and practices of Judaism during the four-hundred-year interlude between the Testaments sheds additional light on, and prepares us for a study of, the New Testament teaching on fasting. As implied by Zechariah:

> In exilic Judaism with its legalistic trends, fasting was one of the most important of religious activities. Up to NT days fasting came to occupy so high a place in the practice and estimation of Judaism that for Gentiles it is one of the marks of the Jew.[1]

The Apocrypha and Pseudepigrapha frequently mention fasting. Judith fasted every weekday except sabbath eve, sabbath and certain other Jewish holy days during her widowhood (Jud. 8:6). Ezra (4 Ezra 6:31), Jeremiah and others (2 Bar. 5:7), Reuben (Test. Reub. 1:10), Judah (Test. Jud. 15:4), Simeon (Test. Sim. 3:4), and Joseph (Test. Jos. 3:4; 4:8) fasted. Other books of this period also told of fasting (I Macc. 3:47; 2 Macc. 13:12; Test. Ben. 1:4).[2]

Writings from this period stress the power of fasting:

Fasting makes atonement for sins of ignorance (Pss. Sol. 3:8). Prayer, fasting, almsgiving, and righteousness are jointly praised in Tobit (Tobit 12:8). But if one fasts and sins again, his humiliation is unprofitable (Ecclus. 34:26).[3]

The Ethiopian *I Enoch* "is ascetical in tone and presents fasting in connection with humility, divine reward, and the idea of heaven." *The Book of Jubilee* and the *Fragment of a Zadokite Work* forbid fasting on the sabbath. Fasting in the Babylonian *Ta'anit* is for the purpose of repentance and humiliation. A fast can merit answers but cannot force God's hand. Community fasts are especially stressed.[4]

Vows were confirmed and penitence expressed through fasting. Virtue and meritoriousness were emphasized. Fasting prepared one for ecstatic experiences. It was believed that fasting "forgives sins and heals diseases, it drives out spirits and has power even to the throne of God."[5]

In addition to obligatory fast days, the pious voluntarily fasted the second and fifth days of the week regularly. Fasts of one, three, seven and forty days' length are recorded. It was not to be observed on the "preparation of the Sabbath and the Sabbath, the preparation of the new moon and the new moon, and the various feasts and festivals." Mourning gestures accompanying fasting were important. If one's prayers were not answered, the fast was often continued until the answer came. Fasting was considered a path to holiness, with individuals who fasted representing the entire nation before God .[6]

It is necessary to our understanding of New Testament thought that in addition to the Judaistic backdrop between the Testaments, we also note the contemporary Hellenistic concept of fasting. Previously, I have noted the practice of fasting preparatory to initiation into the mystery religions of this period. It also played an important role in receiving oracles from deities. In order to commune with the gods one had to be pure through the abstinence from certain foods which contained evil spirits.

Although the Cynics and Stoics did not totally abstain from food, they limited their diet so they might gain inner peace through self-control. Philo taught about the Day of Atonement fast, but he stressed the controlling influence of abstinence upon the individual. He coupled it with perseverance as "the most worthy and most perfect of offering."[1]

Philo wrote of the Therapeutai, who were a group of men and women living in a community near Alexandria, Egypt. They ate only one light meal each day after sundown. Some of them omitted even that one meal for three to six days at a time. Their main pursuits were studying and meditating upon God.[8]

The fasting mentality of Intertestamental Judaism resembled but went beyond the examples of the Old Testament. It assumed a prominent place in the religion of the Jews but lost its initial significance with God. A people who had lost their way were groping in darkness for God through physical denial but with unregenerate hearts.

CHAPTER 7

THE GOSPELS

In the most noteworthy fast in the New Testament, Jesus fasted forty days and nights in the wilderness (Matt. 4:1-11; Mark 1:12, 13; Luke 4:1-14). Luke attributed the entire temptation event to the activity of the Holy Spirit upon Jesus. He, being full of the Holy Spirit, was led into the wilderness by the Spirit and returned from the experience in the power of the Spirit. Both divine purpose and enabling are seen in Luke's narrative. Fasting, as a necessary part of the temptation period, was included in the divine purpose.

I concur with R.V.G Tasker and Joseph Wimmer in associating the temptation of Christ with Israel's forty years in the wilderness. As Wimmer points out, the terminology of Deuteronomy 8:2-5 and that of the synoptic writers in narrating the temptation are similar. Israel was led by the Lord forty years in the desert. The purpose was to humble, test, and discipline them. Israel was called

God's first-born son in juxtaposition with the relationship of Jesus to the Father (Exod. 4:22).

Israel was tested with hunger and thirst (Pss. 78:17-29; 106:13-15), and they failed to trust God for their provision. Their failure is contrasted with the faithfulness of Jesus who refused to turn the stones into bread to satisfy His hunger. He trusted God's provision. Jesus was the obedient Son which God had intended Israel to be.[1]

It it significant that the only three biblical characters who fasted for forty days and nights were Moses, Elijah, and Jesus. While it is difficult to draw parallels from their experiences, the appearance of Moses and Eliiah with Jesus in the transfiguration speaks of their special relationship. Moses and Elijah represent the law and prophets, while Jesus is the fulfillment of both.

In His inaugural address on the mountainside, Jesus united the Jewish triad of piety, almsgiving, praying and fasting (Matt. 6:1-18).[2] He did not command His disciples to give alms, pray or fast, but anticipated these actions. He condemned the current methods and motives and instructed them in the proper manner, motive and reward. He addressed them singularly and collectively, which may imply public and private fasting.

He condemned glory-seeking hypocrites who applied cosmetics to make themselves "look like death" so that others would notice their self-mortification and consider them very religious. Their purpose was to be seen by men, and Jesus condemned that; He did not condemn fasting, but their manner and motive. Thus, their only reward was to be seen by men, for whatever glory that would provide.[3]

Jesus exhorted them to anoint their head and wash their face. The Mishna strictly forbids these on the Day of Atonement, "for washing and anointing were signs of joy, preparations for a feast, and a festive spirit." (*Yoma* 8:1).[4] Jesus' reason was that in anointing the head and washing the face as usual no one would realize they were fasting.

In the Old Testament almost every fast of spiritual significance was explicitly said to have been done "before the Lord" or "unto the Lord." Jesus confirmed this but went beyond it. Fasting is to be done unto the Father and only the Father is to know about it. Wimmer points out the uniqueness of the terminology here: "*Pater sou,* 'thy Father,' referring to God as the Father of someone other than Jesus, is found nowhere else in the New Testament, only here (Mt. 6:4, 6, 18). In the Old Testament it is found only in Dt. 32:6."[5] An intimate relationship between the individual and the Father is implied. Therefore, Jesus taught that fasting is an intimate experience with God alone.

The reward for right fasting is in the future, in contrast with the reward the hypocrites have already received. The reward is not earned by fasting, but is bestowed because of God's goodness. Wimmer gives a beautiful explanation of this New Testament concept of reward:

> The disciple of Jesus was a slave, not a hireling, and as such had no right to a reward: Luke 17:7-10. But as a slave he belonged to the household, and if he still received a reward, it was not strictly due to him, he did not "earn" it, it was a gift.[6]

Jesus treated helping the poor, praying, and fasting as parallel activities. All three are to be done before the

Father, not before men. All are to be done secretly. The reward is an unmerited gift. This pericope, which was used as an early Christian catechism, provides no guidelines for set times, lengths or frequency of these deeds.[7] That is left to individual discretion.

The synoptic gospels record an incident when Jesus was asked why His disciples did not fast while the Pharisees and John's disciples did (Matt. 9:14-17; Mark 2:18-22; Luke 5:33-38). Mark placed this immediately following the scribes questioning His authority to forgive sins and His banqueting with publicans and sinners. Subsequent to the question of fasting, the Pharisees accused Him on two counts of unlawful activity on the sabbath and began to seek means to destroy Him.

Mark's account in the original language implies that the Pharisees and John's disciples were fasting at that very moment. However, we have no way of knowing which Jewish fast was being observed. Jesus did not condemn their fasting. He answered their question with a rhetorical question, "Can the children of the bridechamber fast?" Matthew's account says He asked, "Can the children of the bridechamber mourn?" Then Jesus stated, "When the bridegroom shall be taken from them . . . then they shall fast." That time was a time of celebration, but fasting would be expected of them after Jesus' return to the Father.

The children of the bridechamber were those friends of the bridegroom whose task it was to make the wedding arrangements.[9] They would fast in the days when the bridegroom would be taken away from them. This is the first mention of Jesus' decease. After His ignominious death, fasting would be appropriate. In Matthew 6, Jesus taught that fasting was to be done secretly unto the Father. Here He taught the appropriate time: during His absence, while we await the consummation of His Kingdom.

John's disciples understood the implications because he had referred to Jesus as the bridegroom (John 3:29). The prophets Isaiah, Ezekiel, and Hosea spoke of God as Israel's husband who was betrothed to her forever (Isa. 54:5, 6; Ezek. 16:60; Hos. 2:16-20).

The Pharisees understood the significance of joyous wedding festivities. Jesus' teaching regarding the festive attitude in His presence was implied by Zechariah, as mentioned earlier, and by Isaiah, who prophesied, "The Spirit of the Lord God is upon me; because the Lord hath anointed me to . . . comfort all that mourn; To appoint unto them that mourn in Zion, to give unto them beauty for ashes, the oil of joy for mourning, the garment of praise for the spirit of heaviness" (Isa. 61:1-3). Alfred Edersheim explains the marriage customs as follows:

> By universal consent and according to Rabbinic law, this was to be a time of unmixed festivity. Even on the Day of Atonement a bride was allowed to relax one of the ordinances of that strictest fast. During the marriage-week all mourning was to be suspended—even the obligation of the prescribed daily prayers ceased. It was regarded as religious duty to gladden the bride and bridegroom.[8]

Jesus' reply to His examiners is packed with divine implications.

Immediately following the marriage analogy, Jesus gave a parable relevant to fasting. He asserted that men do not place a new patch on an old garment or fill old wineskins with new wine. The new material had not been pre-shrunk and would strain and tear the old cloth. The old skins would rot as they grow old and the new wine would burst them with fermentation.[10] The old garment and wineskins had served their purpose. New ones were needed. Jesus was saying, in effect, "I have brought a new and living way which is not congruous with the old legalistic way. My disciples will fast, but not be bound by certain required fast days. They will fast spontaneously from their hearts." However, Jesus added, "There will be some who will continue the old way and make fasting an ordinance." (See Luke 5:33-39.)

A later episode in which Jesus condemned the fault-finding generation of His time is recorded in Matthew and Luke (Matt. 11:16-19; Luke 7:31-34). He said they were like children playing games They piped to John and he would not dance. Piping and dancing were part of the wedding celebration. Unlike others, John the Baptist had come out of the wilderness in his camel's-hair clothing, eating locusts and wild honey. He had preached repentence and judgment, but they said he was crazy.[11] They had wanted him to participate in their joyous festivities and he would not.

On the other hand, Jesus attended weddings and banquets. He was a friend of unscrupulous tax collectors and social outcasts. They called Him glutton and wine-bibber for not mourning with them. They may have tired to force their fasting customs upon Jesus. Under the law a son who was a glutton and a drunkard was stoned to death (Deut. 21:20, 21). This was a gross insult toward Jesus.

Another time Jesus spoke of fasting when a multitude had followed Him three days without eating. This was a voluntary act on their part. They could have returned to their homes to eat, but they chose to remain with the Master to hear His words and see His works of healing and deliverance. Jesus did not send them away hungry, but fed them miraculously with bread and fish (Matt. 15:32-38; Mark 8:1-9). In a different account a multitude had followed Jesus one day without food when He fed them in a similar manner (Matt. 14; Mark 6; Luke 9; John 6). By these examples He taught that if man refuses physical bread in order to follow Christ, his spiritual and physical hunger will be filled.

Only Luke recorded the story of Anna the prophetess "who served God with fastings and prayers night and day" (Luke 2:36-38). Although she did not live at the Temple, she spent most of her time there. When Mary and Joseph brought Jesus in to the Temple for the purification rites, Anna immediately recognized the baby as the Redeemer of Israel. No bright star led her, no angels announced the identity of the baby to her, and no miracles had been performed before her, but the Lord revealed to her the identity of the child. Both fasting and praying in this narrative are considered a service unto God. The acts were directed toward God and served God's purposes. Anna did not fast for revelation, but God gave her spiritual insight.

Luke is also the soul source of the parable of the Pharisee and the Publican (Luke 18:9-14). The Pharisee boasted of his fasting and tithing. He fasted almost one-third of the year by observing all prescribed national fast days and by fasting every Monday and Thursday. Not all

Jews or even Pharisees fasted twice every week. Those who did so went beyond the required fasts.

Mondays and Thursdays were special days to Jews because Moses was thought to have ascended Mount Sinai on the fifth day of the week and descended on the second day. Besides the prescribed annual fast-days:

> . . . occasional fasts were from time to time ordered in seasons of drought and other public calamities, and these additional fasts were always held on Mondays and Thursdays. Thus, a five days' fast would not last from Monday to Friday inclusive, but would be held on all Mondays and Thursdays until the live days were made up. [12]

It has already been noted that on only two days a year was the fast a rigid one of twenty-four to twenty-six hours. All others were observed from daybreak to nightfall, after which a meal was taken.

Edersheim points out that Mondays and Thursdays:

> . . . were also the regular market days, when the country-people came to the towns, and there were special Services in the Synagogues, and the local Sanhedrin met—so that these saints in Israel would, at the same time, attract and receive special notice for their fasts. [13]

Jesus declared the Publican, who claimed none of these righteous works, justified before God.'[14] He had not claimed to have fasted or paid tithes. He humbly begged God for mercy. By smiting himself on the breast and saying," God, be merciful to me a sinner," he had kept the most serious part of the Jewish confession on the Day of Atonement.[15]

On the other hand, the Pharisee, who judged all others by his own standard of righteousness was condemned. He was proud of his righteousness, which he thought he had obtained by fasting and tithing. He scorned those who did not achieve his standard, which exceeded the law. Jesus did not disapprove of his fasting and tithing, but his attitude.

According to this account, fasting is worthless if it is done with the wrong spirit. Fasting can become a source of pride and a holier-than-thou attitude. It can give one a sense of false eternal security. It will not in itself justify a person. What God wants is confession and humility.

Another narrative, the healing of the demoniac son, is a difficult biblical passage (Matt. 17:14-21; Mark 9:14-29; Luke 9:37-42). Jesus had descended the mount of the Transfiguration with Peter, James, and John to a multitude congregated about the other nine disciples. They had not been able to cure the demoniac boy because of their lack of faith.

In order to properly understand this passage, we need to remember that Jesus had previously commissioned and given power to the twelve to cast out devils and heal the sick (Matt. 10:8; Mark 6:7; Luke 9:1). They had already exercised that power in other cases. However, in this instance they could not.

Throughout the New Testament, faith is inseparably connected with prayer (Matt. 21:18-22; Mark 11:21-24; James 1:6). Jude suggested that faith is built by praying in the Holy Spirit (Jude 20). Christ is both the instrument and object of faith (John 1:7; 20:30, 31).

Both Jesus and Paul imply that faith is awakened through hearing the preaching of Christ (Luke 17:5, 6; Rom. 10:17). The disciples needed an assurance of the authority which Christ had already imparted to them. It is interesting that after Pentecost the disciples had no problem with impotency of faith. They healed all who were sick and vexed with unclean spirits (Acts 5:15, 16). No mention is made there of previous fasting and prayer.

Matthew 17:21 and Mark 9:29 are the only passages in the King James Version which indicate that this faith comes through prayer and fasting. Matthew 17:21 does not appear in Codex Sinaiticus, Codex Vaticanus, or the ancient Syriac and Egyptian versions.[16] Written in the fourth century, the two codices are the best extant uncial manuscripts and the two versions are among the oldest.[17] The editorial committee of the Nestle-Aland Greek New Testament is practically certain that "and fasting" in Mark 9:29 was not in the original texts.[18] Scholars believe that "and fasting" was added by overzealous copyists in the later manuscripts of Mark to strengthen the doctrinal tradition about fasting or to harmonize with other passages which use both prayer and fasting (Matt. 6; Acts 13:2, 3; 14:23).[19]

"To add to this evidence is the bridegroom passage in which Jesus explained that His disciples would fast after He was taken away. If Jesus rebuked them for their lack of faith due to their laxity in fasting, this passage would conflict with His earlier teaching on fasting. Why would He rebuke them now when He had earlier explained the reason they would not fast in His presence. In light of this data the addition of "and fasting" in Mark and the entire verse in Matthew is dubious in the original texts.

Finally, it is possible that Jesus did not eat the Passover meal with His disciples on the eve of His betrayal. However, we would be grappling for uncertainties if we regarded this as a fast because there is as much evidence that He ate with His disciples as against it (Luke 22: 14-20).

CHAPTER 8

THE NEW TESTAMENT CHURCH
AND THE LETTERS OF PAUL

The earliest fast recorded in New Testament church history is that of Paul at the time of his conversion. The scant details say that he did not eat or drink for three days (Acts 9:9). Fasting was not new to him since he was a Pharisee. This particular fast may have been the result of his traumatic experience on the Damascus Road and his resultant blindness. However, it could be associated with his spiritual experience. After being struck down and blinded by the brilliance of the glorified Savior, he may have fasted in repentant and humble response.

Luke also penned the narrative of Cornelius, a devout man of prayer and almsgiving, who was fasting when God answered his prayer by sending Peter to give him tidings of the gift of the Holy Spirit (Acts 10). In this story the triad of Christian activities as taught by Jesus in His Sermon on the Mount is repeated. Cornelius was a gentile god-fearer who worshiped at the synagogue. At a time when he was fasting, God remembered him for his prayers and generous contributions to the poor (Acts 10:31).

I. Howard Marshall and Joseph Wimmer believe that the best reading of the original text would not include fasting. However, I prefer the decision of the editorial committee of the Nestle-Aland Greek New Testament who show "a very high degree of doubt" concerning the reading which omits fasting.[1]

Luke named five prophets and teachers of the Antioch church who were worshiping the Lord and fasting (Acts 13:1-3). During this time the Holy Spirit directed that two of them, Paul and Barnabas, be set apart for a work to which God had called them. After fasting and prayer, the others laid hands on Paul and Barnabas and sent them forth. We do not know whether the entire church at Antioch was on hand. "They" seems to refer only to the five men named. Verses two and three may be referring to the same fast, or two separate fasts may be indicated. During a time of worshiping and fasting, the Holy Spirit gave a directive, and with this fasting-and- praying background the duo was sent on their first missionary journey. We cannot deduce from this passage that the brethren were seeking guidance; but it was given while they were worshiping God and fasting.

Paul and Barnabas preached the gospel in Cyprus, Perga, Pisidian Antioch, Iconium, Lystra and Derbe. From Derbe they returned to Lystra, Iconium and Pisidian Antioch, and appointed elders to lead the churches established in those places. While praying with fasting, Paul and Barnabas commended the new converts and their leaders to the care and protection of the Lord (Acts 14:23). The missionaries had been persecuted and driven from Antioch to Iconium. From there they fled for their lives to Lystra where Paul was stoned and left for dead. Fear for the saints they had left behind prompted them to pray and fast. These fasts remind us of the Old Testament examples of Ezra, Esther, and others for divine protection.

Similar to King Saul's rash non-religious fast, forty Jews who were determined to kill Paul "bound themselves under a curse, saying that they would neither eat nor drink till they had killed him" (Acts 23:12). T.C. Smith states, "This sort of fanaticism was characteristic of life in Jerusalem among certain terrorists who instigated the revolt against Rome in A.D.66." [2] Nonetheless, Paul's life was preserved.

Acts 27 speaks of fasting three times. The first account (verse 9) mentions "the fast," which is interpreted as the Day of Atonement fast, which was evidently still being observed by Jews. The second (verse 21) and third (verses 33-36) refer to the two-week fast by the passengers and shipmen of the Alexandrian cargo ship which was driven by a violent storm. On the fourteenth day Paul urged them to eat so they would have strength for the ordeal. In verse 21 of the King James Version Paul seems to be fasting, but verse 33 indicates that it was the others who were abstaining. Paul addressed them with the second person plural "you" which excluded himself from the fasting.

No motive is given for their abstinence. Since the ship was carrying grain to Rome, there was sufficient food aboard. It is possible that the work of keeping the ship afloat during the storm was so great that there was no time for eating. On the other hand, they may have fasted to appease the gods so that their lives would be spared. This was common among pagans in times of disaster. Or perhaps they were in such fear for their lives they could not eat. The fast is first mentioned at the point when the sun and stars had been hidden for many days, the storm was raging, and all hope was gone that the ship, its crew, passengers, and cargo might be saved. Without the sun or stars, the crew was unable to navigate the ship, which created a sense of hopelessness.

In the King James Version fasting is mentioned in both of Paul's epistles to the Corinthians. However, some experts believe that fasting was probably not in the original text of 1 Corinthians 7:5.[3] The text should read, "Defraud ye not one the other, except it be with consent for a time, that ye may give yourselves to . . . prayer." The Jewish Mishna which proscribes conjugal intercourse for anyone fasting, may have influenced the addition of the words "and fasting."

In 2 Corinthians 6:4, 5, Paul's hardships as a minister of the gospel are listed. *Nesteiais* is listed among them. This Greek word can be translated in the religious sense of fasting or not eating, whether voluntarily or involuntarily. Tasker, Wimmer and Plummer believe that fasting in the religious sense is inappropriate in a list of hardships since fasting is related to worshiping or serving God. While Tasker and Wimmer interpret 2 Corinthians 11:27 as hunger in a list expressing his ministerial hard- ships, Plummer disagrees. He points out that involuntary hunger and thirst have already been mentioned, so that it would be redundant to translate *nesteialis* as hunger too. He is not sure whether the fastings are for religious purposes or voluntary foregoing of meals in order to accomplish more work.[4]

I disagree with Tasker, Wimmer and Plummer regarding 2 Corinthians 6:4, 5, because the immediate context is not entirely a list of hardships. "Fastings" is situated between the list of hardships and a list of Christian virtues. Therefore, I consider it entirely possible that fastings may be taken in a religious sense. On the latter passage I concur with

Plummer, in that since hunger and thirst are already mentioned, *nesteiais* should be translated fastings. However, I see no reason why it cannot be given religious significance. The sufferings immediately surrounding the word are those to which Paul subjected himself for the sake of the gospel. I would translate it as it is in the King James, "in fastings."

The relative infrequency of fasting in the New Testament church is noticeable. The general attitude of the early church after Pentecost was expressed by Luke in Acts 2:46, 47: "And they, continuing daily with one accord in the temple, and breaking bread from house to house, did eat their meat with gladness and singleness of heart, praising God, and having favor with all the people." However, from the beginning of the church man-made ordinances apparently rivaled Christian liberty.

Fasting continued to play an important role in Judaism. Others were affected by it because Josephus was pleased that other nations had adopted the practice.[5] Incipient gnosticism, with its libertinism on the one hand and asceticism on the other, made inroads into the Christian community. Paul wrote to Timothy, "that in latter times some shall depart from the faith . . . commanding to abstain from meats" (I Tim. 4:1-3). He warned the Colossians:

> Let no man beguile you of your reward in a voluntary humility . . . after the commandments and doctrines of men. Which things have indeed a shew of wisdom in will worship, and humility, and neglecting the body; not in any honour to the satisfying of the flesh (Col. 2:18-23).

Paul informed the Corinthian church of the proper Christian attitude toward food: "But meat commendeth us not to God; for neither, if we eat, are we the better; neither, if We eat not, are we the worse" (1 Cor. 8:8). Although the context of this verse deals with meats offered to idols, it seems that Paul was saying that no matter what kind of meat it is, whether meat offered to idols or not, we will not be brought closer to God if we eat it or if we do not. This answers questions posed by the problem of Jewish legalists and ascetic gnostics who would attempt to impose fasts upon Christians.

Chapter 9

The Ante-nicene Era

Among the Jews, fast days multiplied after the second Temple was destroyed. The last of the ten plagues in Egypt, the death of the first-born sons, was commemorated with a fast. One might also fast following unpleasant dreams, to subdue unfavorable decrees, on one's wedding day, and on other occasions. Following the Hadrianic persecutions (A.D. 132-135), the remainder of the four commemorative fasts were again made obligatory, along with the previously obligatory fast of *Tisha B'Av.*[1]

Dating from the end of the first century to the middle of the second, six of the eight Apostolic Fathers wrote about fasting. About A.D. 96, Clement of Rome associated fasting and humiliation in reviewing the fast of Moses on Sinai and the fast of Judith. It is because of Judith's fasting and humiliation that God delivered her people. Polycarp, friend of the apostle John and bishop of Smyrna, urged the Philippians to be "sober unto prayer and constant in fastings."[2]

The *Didache* exhorts its readers to pray for their enemies and fast for the ones who persecute them. Baptismal candidates were ordered to fast one or two days before their baptism. This is the first ordered fast for Christians. The one who baptized the catechumens and other Christians were also to fast if they were able. The readers of the *Didache* were not to fast as the hypocrites did on Mondays and Thursdays, but on Wednesdays and Fridays.[3]

Barnabas twice repeated Moses' fast of forty days and nights on Mount Sinai. He exhorted his readers to acceptable fasting by quoting Isaiah 58:4-10. He referred to the Day of Atonement which he believed was to be observed by all the people, under punishment of death for eating on that day. He says that the people fasted and wailed in sackcloth and ashes.[4]

Hermas fasted for revelations. Prior to his second vision, he fasted fifteen days. The third came after frequent fastings and begging the Lord. In a night vision an old woman told him that in order to receive revelation he must humble himself by fasting. Hermas began fasting and that very night received a revelation. In a parable he was fasting according to his custom when a shepherd taught him that a complete and acceptable fast was not a vain fast such as his, but was obeying and serving God with an undefiled heart and abstaining from evil. Then he gave a parable about fasting in which he performed more of his master's commandments than was required and received great praise and was made a joint-heir with the master's son. When asked for the meaning of the parable, Hermas was told he had to do more than fast. He had to keep his heart pure, obey the commands of the Lord, abstain from evil, and give his excess to the poor. In this particular fast he was instructed to eat only bread and water and give to the needy the amount he would have spent on meat. This fast is considered humbling the soul.[5]

The *Epistle to Diognetus* criticizes the Jews for the pretense of their fasting. The author called their appointed periods of mourning ridiculous and sheer folly. Their mourning fasts commemorated Jewish disasters. He was glad that the Christians were refraining from this error.[6]

An ancient homily (cir. A.D. 120-140), often attributed to Clement of Rome but of unknown authorship, had this to say about fasting, "Fasting is better than prayer, but almsgiving than both."[7] In 128 Aristides reported to the Emperor Hadrian that Christians fasted two or three days and gave the food saved to the poor. Justin tells that fasting precedes baptism, and the *Apostolic Didascalias* speaks of fasting.[8] In a letter to Pope Victor in 195 concerning the Paschal Controversy, Irenaeus said, "Some fast one, some two or more days of holy week, others forty hours (from the hour of crucifixion to Easter sunrise); this variety of observance is of long standing and existed in the time of our ancestors."[9] From the end of the second century the Muratorian Canon relates that the apostle John asked some fellow-disciples and bishops to fast with him for two or three days to see what would be revealed to them.[10]

About A.D. 208, in his book *On Fasting*, Tertullian opposed the montanists, who refused to keep the Day of Atonement fast. They believed it had been abolished. Instead, they fasted from Good Friday until Easter, in addition to Wednesdays, Fridays and dry-food days in which they abstained from pleasant bread. These were not required, but voluntary fasts. Tertullian believed that abstinence earns the favor of God and reconciles God to man. He extolled it as a weapon to fight the worst devils, and which merits understanding mysteries. It changes the nature, averts perils, and blots out sin.[11]

Hippolytus accused the Montanists of unusual fasts. Besides Tertullian, Clement of Alexandria and James of Nisibis each wrote a book on fasting. Origen praised those who fasted to feed the poor.[12]

The *Constitutions of the Holy Apostles* says that Christ commanded the church to fast for six days in mourning for the Jews who did not believe in Him. He allegedly commanded us to fast on Wednesday and Friday because these were the days of His betrayal and passion. The author asked that the surplus from fasting go to the needy. This same document orders an offender to fast according to the intensity of his sin for a period of two, three, five or seven weeks, but stipulates that those who fast on Easter or during Pentecost commit sin.[13]

Early in the third century Pope Callistus decreed a quarterly fast. The author of *The Vision of Paul* saw people tortured in Tartarus for breaking their fast before the appointed hour. In the *Recognitions of Clement* fasting must precede baptism as we saw in the Didache.[14] On the other hand, in the *Excerpts of Theodotus,* "food makes us neither more righteous nor less."[15]

Near the end of the second century, because of disputes, synods met to determine the length of the Paschal fast which commemorated the crucifixion. A fast was called *statio* by the church because those who fasted had to wait in prayer day and night like a soldier at his post.[16]

A far greater interest in fasting is shown during this period of time than during the New Testament era. Although strands of biblical truth emerged, Christendom quickly lapsed into Jewish legalism and piety. From the *Didache* forward, fasting was ordered and days were specified. It was related to humiliation and guaranteed revelation. It was enjoined for one's enemies, and by and in behalf of baptismal candidates. Proceeds from the food savings were given to the poor. The most popular fast from early times was Passover weekend, which commemorated Christ's death. However, according to the Scriptures, Jesus did not command a fast, but a supper, to commemorate His death.

Not until Tertullian's time was fasting reckoned to earn or merit favor and intervention from God. The *Constitutions* credited Christ with commands to fast which are not in Scripture. The backslider was directed to fast for penance. Quarterly fasts were decreed by the pope, and people were tortured if they broke their fast. Only two of our sources, the *Epistle to Diognetus* and *Eucerpts of Theodotus,* seem indifferent to fasting. As can be seen from these historical records, the practice of fasting became far removed from the biblical intent.

In his *Ecclesiastical History,* Eusebius of Cesarea (cir. A.D. 264-339) related a narrative about the aged apostle John, who, in attempting to restore an erring young man, stayed with him, frequently prayed, and constantly fasted for him until he was reclaimed. The historian also referred to the forty-day fast of Jesus in the wilderness. He quoted Irenaeus' writings from the end of the first century:

"So far are they," says he, "from raising the dead, as the Lord raised, and as the apostles by means of prayer, for even among the brethren frequently as in a case of necessity when a whole church united in much fasting and prayer, the spirit has returned to the examinated body, and the man was granted to the prayers of the saints."[17]

Irenaeus spoke as though casting out demons, healing the sick and raising the dead were the result of a gift freely given to the church. Jesus and the apostles did these things simply through prayer, but the church of Irenaeus' time united in fasting and prayer in order to do the same things.

Eusebius spoke of the Paschal dissensions over fasting beginning in the lifetime of Polycarp and Anicetus because of the differences of opinion regarding the celebration of the Resurrection on which the fast was to cease. Next to the Arian controversy, the establishing of a universal date for Easter each year was the second most important issue of the Nicene Council in A.D. 325. To establish a universal date enabled the church to uniformly observe the fasts and feasts which commemorated the Lord's death and resurrection.[18]

Eusebius again quoted Irenaeus in telling of several leaders of the early church who did not observe the Paschal week with fasting and feasting, and who forbade others to keep it. Although Anicetus tried to persuade Polycarp not to observe the week, the bishop of Smyrna continued to observe it as he reportedly had with the apostle John and the other apostles whom he knew. To no avail Polycarp also tried to convince Anicetus to observe the week.[19]

Eusebius said that Origen (cir. A.D. 185-254) sometimes fasted. He also referred to some discussions on fasting written by Titus Flavius to Clement of Alexandria (cir. A.D. 150-215). The historian did not mention occurences of fasting for a period of about one hundred years, from the beginning of the third century to the beginning of the fourth century. Then he told of some dispersed confessors praying and fasting as a customary duty during a period of persecution.[20]

Chapter 10

The Nicene and Post-Nicene Eras

The Nicene and post-Nicene periods span between one-hundred and one-hundred-fifty years. The lives of most of the men who wrote on fasting overlapped. Whether they were from the East or West, their theology of fasting was much the same. Three of them, Ambrose, Jerome and Augustine, were considered the greatest theologians of their time.

Basil, bishop of Caesarea (cir. A.D. 330-379), said, "Fasting begets prophets, strengthens strong men. Fasting makes lawgivers wise, is the soul's safeguard, the body's trusting comrade, the armour of the champion, the training of the athlete."[1]

St. Ambrose (cir. A.D. 340-397), bishop of Milan, believed that fasting and alms wash away sins. His sentiment toward fasting is revealed in the following statement: "Wherefore also the Lord Jesus, wishing to make us more strong against the temptations of the devil, fasted when about to contend with him, that we might know that we can in no other way overcome the enticements of evil."[2]

St. John Chrysostom believed that Christ left us an example in fasting and that it guards against the devil. He said the apostles were almost constantly fasting. "He that fasts is light and winged, and prays with wakefulness, and quenches his wicked lusts, and propitiates God, and humbles his soul when lifted up."[3]

Jerome's (A.D. 345-420) biblical interpretation commanded binding fasts. Although he was against immoderate fasting, he believed that fasting is pleasing to God, as shown by the Scriptures. In some instances, he copied Tertullian almost verbatim.[4]

Augustine (A.D. 354-430), bishop of Hippo, believed that fasting conquers the body. Although by this time rules regarding fasting had been made in two ecumenical councils (A.D. 325 and 381), they were not strictly obeyed.[5]

St. Leo the Great (cir. A.D. 400-461) was noted for his numerous sermons on fasting. His philosophy was this: There are three things which most belong to religious actions, namely, prayer, fasting, and almsgiving."[6]

St. Peter Chrysologus (A.D. 406-450) believed prayer, fasting, and almsgiving were really one. He said, "Fasting is the soul of prayer, and helping the needy is the life-blood of fasting."[7]

Ambrose, Ephraem, Hilary of Poitiers, Augustine, and Leo the Great taught that Christians should follow Jesus' example in fasting forty days. Epiphanius said that

Christians throughout the whole world were fasting every Wednesday and Friday. One can see how during this period the significance of fasting was intensified. It was becoming the all-encompassing hope of salvation for the soul and body.[8]

CHAPTER 11

THE MEDIEVAL ERA

Medieval writings on fasting are relatively scarce. This period was characterized by the intensification and proliferation of fasting. The obligatory fasting which marked this era was unprecedented in the Christian church.

The Second Council of Orleans (A.D. 541) made fasting obligatory. During the eighth century, fasting was considered meritorious and offenders were excommunicated. Days and periods of fasting increased. Fasts were kept every Friday in commemoration of the Crucifixion. The eve before certain holidays, such as Christmas, Epiphany, Pentecost, and Easter, were fast days, in addition to quarterly fasts. Two extended periods of fasting were observed four weeks before Christmas and forty days before Easter. Although called fasts, these seasons were not observed with fasting in the strictest sense, but by a reduced diet.[1]

Fasting had seized the world like the plague. The number of fasts in the Greek Orthodox Church multiplied to 226 besides private fasts. The Rule of St. Benedict and the Rule of St. Francis prescribed fasts for the monasteries. Maximus, famous for his ascetic works used in the Eastern monasteries, wrote three treatises on fasting. The Cathari, or Albigenses, lived a life of chastity, poverty, and fasting. Often their fasting was carried to the point of suicide. At this time instituting annual Jewish fast days became very popular. Under Pope Innocent III, one of the responsibilities of the priests on Sunday was to announce the fast days.[2]

St. Thomas Aquinas taught that the reasons for fasting were to control lust, atone for sins and free the mind for contemplation. The Christian could have minor sins cleansed by daily fasting, praying, and almsgiving. Monks sometimes fasted against an offender. With this rigidity of fasting customs came abuse. If a person had the money, he could buy exemption from abstinence. During the thirteenth century, England proclaimed special fasts due to a threat of famine. The purpose of the fast was to appease God's wrath.[3]

The practice of fasting with its implication of mourning was appropriate for this dark age (approximately 500-1500) of chaos, conflict, decadence and disaster. The spirit of the age may explain the proliferation of obligatory fast days. Perhaps, by fasting, the world mourned and repented for its loathsome condition.

CHAPTER 12

THE REFORMATION AND POST-REFORMATION ERAS

Private Fasting

The great leaders of the Reformation and Protestantism sought by example and instruction to correct the abuses of fasting during the Middle Ages and to restore its original biblical intention. Martin Luther (1483-1546) rejected the strict requirements of the church which caused people to believe fasting would justify them. He taught "that genuine Christian fasting is a fruit of repentance, that it helps keep the flesh in check and is a fine outward training in preparing to better receive God's grace." He fasted intermittently while translating the Bible. At one point in his life, friends thought his health was endangered due to much fasting.[1]

Italian reformer Girolamo Savonarola (1452-1498) grew so weak from fasting that he had to be assisted to remain in the pulpit. His powerful sermons were so effective that his audience wept while beating their breasts and crying for God's mercy. His sermons caused such fear that the streets of Florence were silent.[2]

The Scottish reformer John Knox (cir. 1505-1572) was the greatest single influence upon his nation and its religion. He was also a man of fasting and prayer.[3]

John Calvin (1509-1564) exposed the abominable fasting habits of the Catholic Church in his time. Because animal food was forbidden, choice delicacies in abundant supply were consumed in the pretense of abstinence. Some of the most outwardly pious were more gluttonous during seasons of fasting than during the rest of the year. Although Calvin admitted to the wisdom of early Church Fathers, he blamed the sixteenth-century abuses on their extreme praise of abstinence. Fasting is of no value to God unless the heart is right and unless fasting is accompanied by genuine repentance, humiliation, and sorrow in the presence of an awesome God. Calvin believed that Jesus did not abolish fasting altogether but assigned it to periods of distress.[4]

By the late 1600's, Matthew Henry (1662-1714) was expressing regret that fasting was generally neglected among Christians of his day. He assumed that it was a duty required of believers. The pastor and scholar listed four reasons why fasting is important: it secures God's power to assist us; it sharpens prayer; it demonstrates humiliation before God; it controls the body.[5]

Jonathan Edwards (1703-1758), pastor of Northampton, Massachusetts, was a leader of the Great Awakening in New England. Throngs attended his meetings in which his sermons were accompanied by fainting and outcries. Many communities were spiritually changed. He fasted three days prior to the revival in which he preached his powerful sermon, "Sinners in the Hands of an Angry God." He interceded repeatedly for New England. When he arose from praying and entered the pulpit, his countenance reflected God's presence. The congregation was moved even before he spoke. During the sermon one man ran down the aisle toward him asking, "Mr. Edwards, is there no mercy with God?" Others clung to their pews for fear of falling into destruction.[6]

The founder of Methodism, John Wesley (1703-1791), preached and practiced fasting. The members of the Holy Club of Oxford, which he founded fasted each Wednesday and Friday. He later encouraged all Methodists to observe the same days, because he believed that the early church kept these days. He refused to ordain a man into the Methodist ministry who would not fast until 4 P.M. every Wednesday and Friday.[7]

Henry Gallus gave examples of the strictness with which Wesley taught fasting. The English clergyman is reported to have said that one who never fasts will no more enter heaven than one who never prays. He also believed that Christians cannot abstain from sin without fasting. Wesley would rather consider cursing than omit his regular Wednesday and Friday fasts. He said that if he failed to fast and pray, he quickly lost his spiritual fervor.[8]

Wesley's sermon on the subject states that fasting is to be done unto the Lord for these purposes: to glorify God; show our sorrow for our sins; wait for purifying grace to turn our attention toward heavenly things; add earnestness to our supplications; prevent God's wrath; and obtain all the promises of God. Abstinence does not merit salvation or blessings. "Fasting is only a way which God hath ordained, wherein we wait for His unmerited mercy; and wherein, without any desert of ours, He hath promised freely to give us His blessing."[9]

The missionary David Brainerd (1718-1747) and the evangelist William Bramwell (1759-1818) were fasting men. Brainerd set aside a day to fast and pray in preparing for his ministry. Bramwell fasted to conquer the attachment to earthly goods.[10]

Men of the nineteenth-century who were given to fasting were Charles G. Finney (1792-1875), Andrew Murray (1828-1917), and Charles H. Spurgeon (1834-1892). When Finney felt devoid of the power of God, he would fast and pray for a day. When he had humbled himself and begged God for help, the power was restored. Murray said that fasting validates our claim to sacrifice anything for our requests in behalf of the kingdom of God. Spurgeon once announced, "Our seasons of fasting and prayer at the Tabernacle have been high days indeed; never has Heaven's gate stood wider; never have our hearts been nearer the central Glory."[11]

Public Fasting

In addition to the fasting experiences of leading individuals, historical records afford us seven interesting accounts of public fasts which were called either by ecclesiastical leaders or heads of state. Calvin assigned the task of public fast days to pastors in times of necessity. These special periods of supplication were to avert the wrath of God. He recommended that when an entire country suffered from war, pestilence or other calamity all the people should repent of their sins.

England observed such special fast days. In 1543 a revolt brought an order for a fast in Yorkshire. In 1563 the men of London were ordered to fast and pray until a plague subsided. Again in 1572 a public fast was announced in London when news arrived of the massacre of scores of Huguenots by Roman Catholics in large French cities. In 1605 a time of fasting and thanksgiving was ordered when the king of England and a number of members of Parliament escaped assassination when the Gunpowder Plot was uncovered. During the 1640's, when the Dissenters gained control of the House of Commons, a monthly day of fasting was appointed; but from 1660 on, public fast days were once again ordered only at times of crises.[13]

A seventeenth-century English official, Samuel Pepys, recorded eighteen special fast days within a decade. One took place on "Wednesday the 30th January 1661 as a sign of the nation's repentance for the 'murder' of Charles I, the late king." On June 10, 1702, the eruption of the War of the Spanish Succession was cause for a fast. Various other general fasts were observed during wars, rebellions, earthquakes, and plagues. In the United Kingdom, the last known appeal for a special fast—during a cholera epidemic in 1853—was refused by Lord Palmerston.[14]

On these solemn days, the people rose early to pray and spent most of the day in church reading and listening to the Word, singing psalms, and receiving offerings for the needy. On that day no rich apparel or ornaments were worn. The Church of England eventually prepared a form of prayer to be used on these special days. It was a prayer to be used:

> . . . in all Churches and Chapels throughout
> . . . Great Britain . . . upon Wednesday the

Ninth of January next, 1740, being the
day appointed by Proclamation for a
General FAST and Humiliation . . . For
obtaining Pardon of our Sins, and for
averting those heavy Judgments which our
manifold Provocations have most justly
deserved; and imploring his Blessing and
Assistance on the Arms of His Majesty
and for restoring and perpetuating Peace,
and Safety, and Prosperity to Himself, and
to His Kingdoms.'[15]

Not everyone was in favor of the public fasts. The
founder of the Quakers, George Fox (1624-1691),
recommended only private fasting in times of distress.[16]

Other countries also proclaimed public fasts. The
miserable aftermath of the Thirty Years' War caused the
elector of Saxony (Germany) John George I, to order a
day of repentance and prayer in 1633. The king of Prussia
announced a fast in 1870 at the eruption of the Franco-
German War.[17]

America's rich heritage of fasting began before the
pilgrims left the Old World. In preparation for their
hazardous voyage three fasts were held. While they sought
refuge in Holland early in 1620, they fasted for divine
guidance. The second fast day was held after their decision
to sail to America. The third was observed just before
their departure.[18]

Once in the New World, William Bradford, governor
of New England, set aside July 16, 1623, as a day for
humiliation and prayer because an extended drought
threatened their crops. On that very evening a steady rain

soaked and refreshed the corn and favorable weather continued so that in the autumn there was a fruitful harvest.[19]

On November 15, 1636, a law was made permitting the governor and his administrative aids to appoint fast days and days for thanksgiving. Likewise Massachusetts, Connecticut, Maine, and New Hampshire ordered special days of humiliation in case of droughts, plagues, epidemics, Indian wars, earthquakes, or religious apathy. For some states annual days became fixed. These days were passed in two church services which lasted most of the day. No food was eaten until late afternoon.[20]

Massachusetts appointed a fast on February 26, 1740, because King George's War threatened New England shipping. Newport, Rhode Island, held a public fast during the Stamp Act controversy. On May 24, 1774, the Burgesses of Virginia ordered a day of fasting, humiliation and prayer for June 1, the day a British embargo on the port of Boston, Massachusetts, was to commence. George Washington, a Burgess of Virginia at the time, attested the observance of the day. According to his diary, he fasted all day and went to church at the parish church of Bruton in Williamsburg (see Appendix A).[21]

During the Revolutionary War (1775-1783), the Americans and British proclaimed numerous fast days. Congress appointed the following days: July 20, 1775; April 22, 1778; and May 3, 1781. England observed December 13, 1776, February 26, 1778; February 10, 1779; and, February 21, 1781. The second president of the United States, John Adams, ordered a fast for May 9, 1798, in the midst of the French-American conflict. He asked that the day be observed in humiliation, fasting and prayer. It was to be a day of rest, repentance for manifold transgressions, reformation, and supplications for divine forgiveness, favor and protection (see Appendix B).[22]

During the British invasion of 1814, the two Houses of Congress requested a day of public fasting and prayer. The fourth president, James Madison, proclaimed such an event to take place on January 12, 1815 for confessing sins and transgressions, for reformation and thankfulness, and for supplication for peace and guidance for the nation (see Appendix C).[23]

During the Civil War (1861-1865) Abraham Lincoln proclaimed three separate days for humiliation as requested by one or both branches of Congress. Each of these fast days was to be observed by all people either at church or at home. Secular pursuits were to be halted for the day. (See Appendices D, E, and F.)

Two other Civil War fasts were proclaimed. One was held November 21, 1860, lust before the war broke out and the other, which was appointed by a governor of one of the states, was held on April 13, 1865 at the close of the war. Then, after about two and one-half centuries of public fasts, the practice declined. Special days were still observed, but fasting was excluded after the middle of the nineteenth-century.[24]

CHAPTER 13

THE MODERN ERA

Today few governments or religious organizations have laws which require the observance of regular fast days. In the United States, New Hampshire has maintained the fourth Thursday in April as an annual fast day. Prussia and most states in North Central Germany keep the Wednesday before the last Sunday after Trinity.[1]

Only the Day of Atonement fast is obligatory in Reform Judaism. Other than the observance of this day Jews are negatively inclined toward public or private fasting. In the 1960's the Roman Catholic Church changed its fasting and abstinence laws. Now meat can be eaten every Friday except during Lent, and the only fast days are Ash Wednesday and Good Friday. Methodists have no fasting rules such as their founder introduced. Mormons eat only one meal on the first Sunday of each month and give the money saved to the poor. Muslims, as has already been mentioned, fast the month of Ramadan from sunrise to sunset.[2]

The Lutheran Church keeps no fast days per se but appoints days for penance and prayer. Although the Prayerbook of the Church of England contains a list of fast days, no strict rules are made for their observance. According to the *New Schaff-Herzog Encyclopedia*, only the Greek Church "still observes, besides the four great seasons of fasting, also the vigils of the Epiphany, St. John Baptist's day and Holy Cross day, and the weekly fast on Wednesday and Friday; so that half the year is spent in fasting."[3]

Now, more than at any other time in history, fasting is left to the discretion of the individual. Numerous articles in religious magazines and some books on the subject have been published. This century has developed its own distinctive experiential theory about fasting. Phenomenal results have been attributed to its practice.

Norman Grubb, in his book *Rees Howells Intercessor*, speculated that the Battle of Britain in World War II was won by the prayers and fastings of Rees Howells and the students at the Swansea Bible College in Wales. In his book *Shaping History through Prayer and Fasting*, Derek Prince stated his belief that the history of North Africa, Israel, Russia, and Kenya was changed due to prayer and fasting Henry Callus credits fasting by evangelist Gayle Jackson for five-hundred people receiving the gift of the Holy Spirit in one service. David R; Smith attributes the healing of Choi Han Gee, who had become mentally deranged during solitary confinement, to the fasting and prayers of a Presbyterian missionary in Korea,

Bruce F. Hunt. There is a Full Gospel Prayer Mountain in Korea where literally thousands of Pentecostals have gone for seasons of fasting and prayer. Ja Shil Choi says that incurable diseases have been healed, "marriages restored; children and parents reconciled; tormented minds set free; and Satan's bonds loosed because of fasting."[4]

Various theories about fasting are projected by contemporary scholars. Some of these theories are biblical and some of them are philosophical conclusions derived from observations of personal experiences. Ja Shil Choi believes that the principle reason for fasting is to change us so the Holy Spirit can use us in a more dynamic way. Pastor F. Viljoen said that "the power and efficacy of prayer is multiplied many times through fasting." In his book *The Fasting Prayer*, Franklin Hall stated that fasting produces faith. Gordon Lindsay proposed that prayer and fasting are the master keys to the impossible. David R. Smith listed eight benefits of fasting: one can receive guidance, grow in grace, increase in faith, have power over evil, have unction in preaching, possess physical well-being, have power over carnality, and cope with crisis. Arthur Wallis wrote in his book *God's Chosen First* that the purposes of fasting are personal consecration, to have prayers answered, to change God's mind, to set captives free, for deliverance, for revelation, and to keep the body under control. J. Harold Smith recommended fasting for physical, mental, and spiritual well-being.[5]

Gallus considered that "fasting is above all an act of worship and a sacrifice in the deepest sense." The theme of James Lee Beall's book *The Adventure of Fasting* is an inner focus of the heart upon God. Joseph F. Wimmer noted that "fasting acts as an instrument of purification, of penance, and as a test of faith." George A. Maloney, in *A*

Return to Fasting, said fasting produces humility which causes us to live properly towards God, our neighbor, and the universe.[6]

In preparation for this book I surveyed 265 Pentecostals regarding their fasting habits. The group included 127 lay people (mostly women) and 138 preseminary students and ministers (mostly men). (See Appendix G) which is a copy of the questionnaire.) These Pentecostals represent almost all of the fifty states and some other countries. Only two ministers and three lay persons had never fasted. Among the rest, the most popular length of fast was one day. Most of them fast when God impresses them or when their spiritual leader asks them. Twenty-two ministers had fasted for one week or more; four for two weeks or more; two for three weeks; and two for forty days. Of the lay people only eight had fasted one week or more; one for twenty days; and one for twenty-nine days. The two main concerns in their fasting were lost souls and finding the will of God. Sixteen percent more ministers fasted to find the will of God than for lost souls. Twenty percent more lay persons fasted for lost souls than to find the will of God. A total of 223 said they received the answers or results intended. Two-hundred twenty-seven continued their work while they fasted. Most of them read their Bible end prayed during a fast. Almost all drink water or other liquids while fasting. Ninety-seven percent felt closer to the Lord during or following a fast. Seventy-six percent were more mentally alert. Sixteen percent had experienced visions. Of the ministers, fifty-one percent had experienced unusual phenomena, while only thirty-eight percent of the lay people had such experiences.

CHAPTER 14

CONCLUSIONS ON FASTING IN THE
BIBLE AND IN HISTORY

Like a scarlet thread woven the length of a linen garment, fasting has endured from ancient history to the present. Since the earliest biblical command to fast, mourning, repentance, humility, and petition have been closely related to fasting. Especially throughout biblical history, but also in secular history, these themes have emerged when other superficial and erroneous ideas faded.

According to the custom of the day, David and others fasted in mourning over the death of Saul and Abner. Ezra, Nehemiah, Esther, and all of Israel fasted in mourning in moments of urgent crisis. The only two fasts God explicitly ordained, the Day of Atonement fast and Joel's fast, were repentant fasts. Other repentant fasts are recorded in the books of Exodus, Deuteronomy, Judges, 1 Samuel, Nehemiah, Daniel, Joel, and Jonah. Fasting is associated with humility on the Day of Atonement, in the fasts of Ahab, David, and Daniel, and in Israel's fasts as recorded in 1 Samuel, Ezra, and Isaiah. Israel, led by Ezra petitioned

God for traveling mercies. Under King Jehoshaphat, Israel petitioned God for victory in battle. David prayed for the healing of his sick child and sick enemies.

Modern scholars have proposed various motives for the fasts of Moses and Elijah, but the conjectures cannot be validated by the Scriptures. Moses' second fast clearly was in repentance for Israel, but the Bible gives no motive for his first fast. Further, one can only relate the fasts of Moses and Elijah with that of Jesus in noting the special relationship of the three in biblical revelation.

As defined in the beginning of this book, the act of religious fasting itself is to voluntarily abstain from food. In the rare biblical cases of Moses, Elijah, Ezra, Esther, and Paul, water was also omitted. Since no one can live without water more than a few days, Moses and Elijah must have been supernaturally sustained during their fasts. In all other biblical fasts water is assumed to have been taken.

Fasting in the Old Testament was predominately public and for corporate concerns. Either the entire congregation of Israel assembled in fasting, or individuals such as Moses, Ezra, Nehemiah, and Daniel interceded for Israel by fasting. The collective fasts were proclaimed by either the spiritual leader or the political leader. The only recorded private fasts observed for personal needs were those of David and Ahab.

The two fasts God ordained for His people were about twenty-four to twenty-six hours in duration. Most all other fasting was done from sunrise to after sunset. Moses, Elijah, Jesus, Esther and the Jews of Shushan, Daniel, Paul, and possibly the Ninevites, are exceptions. Moses, Elijah, and Jesus fasted forty consecutive days and nights (Moses possibly fasted eighty consecutive days and nights). Daniel fasted three weeks continuously. Esther and the Jews of Shushan and the apostle Paul fasted three days and nights. The Bible does not record the duration of the Ninevites' fast.

In connection with fasting, God appointed the Day of Atonement as a sabbath of rest. On that day work carried a more serious penalty than eating. In the subsequent public fasts, waiting or sitting "before the Lord" was very important. Either "before the Lord" or "unto the Lord" is descriptive of most Old Testament accounts of fasting. Total attention was given to God. If abstaining from work included not feeding the animals, their lowing reminded Israel of the gravity of their need for repentance and humiliation. On that day the income from one's livelihood was also sacrificed.

Either explicitly or implicitly, prayer accompanied the Old Testament fasts. On one occasion Nehemiah reported that Israel read the law for one-fourth of the day and prayed another fourth.

The pattern for fasting in the Old Testament included humbling or afflicting oneself, wearing sackcloth and ashes, weeping, repentance, confession, prayer, separating oneself from the cares of this life, remaining before the Lord, and reading the Scriptures. Initially sackcloth and ashes were the outward symbols of mourning (Gen. 37:34). But gradually these symbols also became the expression of repentance (Matt. 11:21; Luke 10:13). These external signs of mourning became the symbols of sorrow for both sin and death.

On the Day of Atonement, fasting was not "the" atonement for sins. It was a part of the total process for obtaining forgiveness for the sins of the past year and being reconciled with God. Sacrifices were the instruments of atonement for sins. Through the prophet Isaiah, God pointed out to Israel that fasting was not a substitute for repentance and tight living. Fasting had become a stumbling-stone to genuine repentance and obedience. God did not recognize the vain fasts of Israel in Isaiah's or Zechariah's time because the people were not loving God and their fellow man in word and deed.

God promised Israel light, health, protection, answers to prayers, guidance, sustenance in drought, strength, productive and unfailing reservoirs, the restoration of their nation, and an inheritance if they would live according to His people humbled themselves before God with genuine repentance, God responded with protection, guidance, revelation,deliverance,and assistance. Clearly, God responds to a people who are reconciled to himself and others. Fasting with humiliation and repentance was the instrument of reconciliation.

It is unfair to the integrity of the Old Testament to imply that God acted for His people in extra-ordinary ways only when they fasted. Prophets such as Isaiah and Jeremiah had visions and nothing is said about them fasting. The Lord revealed numerous truths to other Old Testament prophets who performed miracles, but few have left a record of fasting. God protected Israel with the cloud and pillar of fire. The Red Sea rolled back, water poured from the rock, manna fell from heaven, fire came down from God, and battles were won without the slightest mention of fasting.

According to the New Testament, Jesus condemned the method and motives of contemporary Judaistic fasting. He rejected the external display of fasting for the glory of men. The fasts of the Pharisees were acts of pride, precisely the opposite of humility, which was the original intent of Scripture concerning fasting. Jesus retained the primary Old Testament objective for fasting: it is to be done unto the Lord. He emphasized the intimate experience of the believer with the Father. He spoke of an unmerited reward for those who fast with the right motives and in the right manner. He treated fasting, almsgiving, and prayer as parallels. That these three were to be done secretly implies individual responsibility. The time for believers to fast is in the interim between His death and His return. Fasting is not to be legalistic; it is to spring spontaneously from the heart of His people. It will not justify a person.

Luke considered fasting part of worship and service unto God. He told of Anna who served the Lord with prayers and fastings, and the Antioch brethren who worshiped and fasted before the Lord. Paul and Barnabas prayed and fasted for the care and protection of infant churches. Although Paul fasted often, his motive is not recorded.

When the Old and New Testament doctrines are integrated, method and motives emerge. Abstention from food and sometimes water constitutes the act itself. The time for fasting is until Christ's return. The length and frequency are individual matters. There is no New Testament prescription. One may fast assembled in unity in response to public proclamations, but private spontaneous fasting is to be done secretly. If possible one should separate himself from the cares of life and remain in God's presence, as "before the Lord," "unto the Lord," and "secretly" imply.

All biblical fasting was done for one or more of five different reasons: mourning for sins; mourning in death; repentance for reconciliation with God; humbling or chastening oneself (body, mind, spirit and petition.) Petition was made for guidance, victory in battle, protection forgiveness for others' sins, understanding, and healing.

The public and private fasts of the Old Testament can be divided into four kinds. Israel fasted during God-ordained, obligatory days. They fasted voluntarily in times of trouble. They also imposed commemorarive public fasts upon themselves. Individuals voluntarily fasted in times of distress. All New Testament fasting by Christians was voluntarily performed publicly or privately.

According to both Testaments, fasting is an act of humility in which one may serve or worship God. Weeping, mourning, repentance, confession, and petition may be involved. It is a time of examining one's life and expressing sorrow and repentance for sins. It is a time for petitioning God with one's requests. Scripture reading may accompany the act. Since moderation is the spirit of the Word, it would seem to apply to fasting.

Three Old Testament ingredients are omitted from the New Testament teaching on fasting. These are the accompanying sacrifices for atonement and the wearing of sackcloth and ashes. The involuntary obligation is also anulled by Jesus' teaching.

In the New Testament many people were healed, devils were cast out, and other divine assistance was given without mention of fasting. Therefore, fasting should not be exalted as the only ultimate means of mighty deeds. However, an undefined, unmerited payment will be given for biblical fasting.

Soon after the biblical era, Christians were ordered to fast, just as Jewish leaders had earlier prescribed fasts. The Catholic Church placed binding restrictions upon the people so that fasting was necessary for forgiveness of sins. Not until the Great Reformation of the sixteenth century was there a revival in genuine Christian fasting. Later the British and United States governments proclaimed public fasts in times of crisis, reflecting the biblical perspective.

It is apparent that fasting was more popular in some centuries than others. It seems that those periods in history when spiritual darkness was greatest fasting was the most misunderstood and abused. When fresh revelation dawned upon the world, biblical fasting was restored to its proper place.

Some basic dangers regarding fasting are to be avoided. Fasting is not a means by which one can manipulate God. It is wrong to think that if we fast, God will do anything we want. Fasting is not a substitute for true repentance. It will not justify one before God. Judging others spiritually inferior who do not fast is the height of pride, which is opposite to the humility related to biblical fasting.

In this century some authors have misunderstood the purpose of fasting and given it some of the credit which belongs to God. Miraculous intervention is not dependent upon fasts; God is eternally the source of all mighty deeds. God alone, not fasting, deserves all the praise and glory for His manifold blessings. The effect of fasting is not upon God although it is before Him and unto Him and fulfills His divine purpose. God does not need the fast; we do. The effect is upon us for our humbling that we may continually live according to His words.

No divine fasting formula states, "Fast-and-ask equals God's response." Rather, live a consistent Christian life, fast in humility before the Lord, and His response will naturally result. According to the scriptural passages examined, the emphasis is not upon the gift, but upon the Giver. If fasting is done primarily unto the Giver, the blessings will automatically result. If we keep His ways, He will keep ours. He responds spontaneously to a reconciled people.

Rather than to view fasting as a means of power beyond prayer, we should see that the power of God is constantly available, and that through fasting we have finally surrendered ourselves to the power of God. Prior to this surrender we had not realized this power, because of our lack of attention toward God.

I believe that the presence of the Lord during or following a fast is not due to the Lord's pouring out or intensifying His presence, but due to one's awareness and alertness to His abiding presence. In personal fastings I have been more aware of my own shortcomings and more aware of God's strength, presence, guidance, and power working in me. Even in the night, when aroused from sleep, the awareness of His presence was much greater than when I was not fasting. I was more in control of my thoughts and actions during the fasting. Finally, in fasting I had come to Him in such a way that I could hear His sweetest whisper and see His sovereign hand at work.

CHAPTER 15

PERSONAL FASTING TESTIMONIES

Before concluding, I want to challenge you with contemporary witnesses of fasting experiences and results. I have written, called, or spoken to about two dozen Christian friends concerning their fasting experiences. Some of them have responded with personal stories; others have recalled the experiences of a friend or family member; and still others have remembered a local congregation's fasts.

I have agreed not to use any names, in keeping with the spirit of Christ's teaching concerning secret fasting and due to the very personal nature of the events. However, I can say that all of the respondents are from a traditional Pentecostal background. I have interviewed about one-half dozen retired ministers, and another half-dozen ministers who serve their church internationally. Others are pastors, minister's wives, college instructors, or businessmen.

Although some witness to more fantastic results than others, I have learned something valuable from each. All conclude that fasting adds a spiritual dimension to their Christian living that is not available through any other means. All conclude that fasting is never worthless. It is always visited with the divine presence. Although the motives vary, this personal discipline always accomplishes God's intended goals. His goals are not always concurrent with the requests of the individual, but supersede them. They are always better, more wonderful, and last longer than finite reason expects.

All of these incidents have occurred within the last fifty years, with a number of them within the last few years. The earlier results are no more spectacular than recent ones.

All of the fasting results which I have received fall into ten major categories:

1. Self-discipline and spiritual growth
2. Church growth
3. Financial needs supplied
4. Spontaneous revivals
5. Miracles of healings
6. Miracles of salvation
7. Church problems solved
8. Divine wisdom and direction given
9. Acts of divine judgment
10. Supernatural visitations of the divine presence, ministering angels, and visions.

Some of these results are bound up together in one glorious event to bring about God's answer for His beloved people. However, we will as often as possible for the sake of clarity stick to the preceding order.

Self-discipline and Spiritual Growth

One international church figure related that he enjoys a sense of accomplishment in bringing the flesh under control through fasting. This self discipline allows the Spirit of God to flow through him more freely.

A pastor noted that he conquered food addiction and gained control of his life in personal devotions, in family devotions, in visitation, in the use of his time, and over timidity through fasting. His time multiplied, his study life was more intense, and his preaching was more fervent. Although he was weak and had to rest periodically through the day, he was able to perform more ministerial duties than usual.

Another minister said that after ten days of fasting he did not want to stop, because the blessings of the Lord were so wonderful. He was more anointed in preaching and had a continual song in his heart. Problems and cares of this earth did not bother him as they did before.

A friend of mine said that she never makes petitionary fasts, but fasts only as a conditioner and cleanser for the ministry. Her attitude about this self-discipline is that it is much like the Old Testament priests preparing to go into the presence of God in the tabernacle. While she makes no particular requests before the Lord, she has a constantly fruitful ministry and has been instrumental in bringing many to Christ. Her ministry has witnessed blind eyes healed, deaf ears opened, tumors and cancer healed, many inner healings, and other deliverances.

Another friend wrote that the purpose of his fast is personal consecration. He said, "I am not trying to get the Lord to do my will, but rather to find His will. I want to be changed into His likeness. I want to be able to say, 'Yes, Lord.' I want to be genuine with no guile. I want to be a clean vessel, useful to Him." On the fifth day of a ten-day fast, he remarked, "I am in a precious state of mind. Oh, what precious communion with the Lord."

On the ninth day he exclaimed, "It is impossible to describe the many benefits these days of fasting have wrought! There is a genuine awareness that God is Jehovah infinitely and eternally, and I am less than nothing!" This man's spouse remarked that he has never been the same since his first extended fast. Other spouses of fasters have confirmed her conclusion, noting remarkable changes in the life and ministry of their partner.

Church Growth

Two pastors have discussed extended fasts with me. Both had accepted mission churches with very small membership. Following extended fasts, the churches began to grow spiritually, numerically, and financially. One of these pastors accepted a church in a new field with nine members. He labored to build the church for several months, but his labors seemed largely unproductive. The membership only grew from nine to sixteen. Then he went on a thirty-four-day fast. It was not for the purpose of building the church, but to get closer to the heart of God and to gain clarity of direction concerning his ministry. The end result included an increase in membership from sixteen to fifty-one several months later. He also mentioned the convicting power of God was much stronger in the services, the church experienced greater unity, and one woman was healed of cancer.

This young minister shared some other blessings and insights he derived from this fast. For him personally, the gray area disappeared and there came a great distinction between right and wrong Spirit and flesh. The flesh was conquered after the fourth day. Carnality died. In the early days of the fast, his main communication with God was praying in the Spirit with groanings, while as the fast progressed it became more and more meditation on God's Word. He became more sensitive and alert to God's gentle promptings, and gained wisdom and a clearer understanding of his role as a shepherd. He petitioned the Lord with four requests during the fast, two of which have been definitely answered, and two which have been assured. He did warn of an unusual battle with lust during the latter days of the fast, but emphasized the conquering power of God over fleshly desires.

A seasoned evangelist, pastor, and international church figure approached a ministerial crisis in his life with a forty-day fast. He worked every day during this fast, but declined all preaching invitations except one funeral. From the very first day he basked in the divine presence. On the seventh, fourteenth, twenty-first, and thirtieth days, he experienced spiritual visions too sacred and intimate with God to speak about. On the fortieth day an angel of the Lord came into his room and laid a hand upon his shoulder. The Lord said, "I've heard your prayers and seen your tears. Commit yourself into my hands without hesitation. Submit your will to me and I will reveal what my will is."

Later, as he and his wife prayed together, the Lord

spoke to both of them at once telling them to accept a pastorate in a specific place. He knew this church was almost defunct. The people were scattered and disillusioned. The average attendance in Sunday School was twenty-six, with monthly tithe and offerings of between twelve hundred and fifteen hundred dollars. But he called the overseer and consented to take the church. About two years later his attendance was 2,763 and monthly tithe and offerings were about $91,000.

This same man shared another very interesting event which occurred on the fortieth day of his fast. While attending a large annual conference he was asked to greet the congregation. He had not been planning to preach because he had lost fifty pounds and was very thin and weak. But as he began to speak, an awesome, powerful anointing came upon him. While he prayed, a large number of people received salvation and the Holy Spirit. As the people rejoiced, he asked everyone to stand who needed a physical healing. He asked them to lay their left hand on the place of their affliction if possible. As they prayed, hundreds of people were healed of cancer, tumors, goiters, and other diseases. Wheelchairs were emptied and people walked. He commented that it was one of the most electrifying experiences of his entire life.

Throughout his fast he shared a common fasting experience of keen sensitivity to the presence of God, an alertness of mind, wisdom to answer questions while people were still speaking and an amazing inspiration. The spiritual blessings of the fast were so outstanding that he mentioned the accompanying physical distress only when I questioned him. The first three days had been the most difficult, with occasional periods of weakness and dizziness.

As a veteran of the fasting discipline, he encourages others to try shorter fasts before going into the longer ones. During his early ministry he had fasted a week at a time while preaching revivals, but later realized it is wisest to prepare himself between revivals.

One remark is necessary here. Neither the young minister nor the seasoned minister fasted specifically for church growth, but God gave the increase along with other results.

Financial Needs Supplied

Three who responded to my fasting inquiries had witnessed God's financial provision after fasts. One told of several times during the depression when much needed groceries and money were brought to their home by people off the street whom they had never seen. This awe-inspiring experience was baffling to this young son of a fasting, praying father.

In the forties a young minister and his wife were sent to a mission state. After several months of receiving financial assistance from the mission department, they were suddenly informed that the funds were depleted. They began fasting and praying. They told no one of their plight, and God provided from unexpected sources. One childhood friend, whom he had not heard from for many years, sent a check with the explanation that the Lord had impressed him to send it. Many others were prompted by the Lord to hand them an offering.

Most recently, following a ten-day fast, one person went into a spiritual slump. He was disappointed that he had experienced no apparent spiritual or other visible benefits from the fast. He became very discouraged. But in three or four days some wonderful things began to happen. They were very low financially. His wife went to the mailbox and found a hundred-dollar bill in it without a note or name. This was a direct answer to prayer. God had waited but had not failed. In another place I will share other results of this fast.

Spontaneous Revival

A retired pastor quickly recalled a time in which he could not secure an evangelist for a revival. He had exhausted every effort to have a revival. He and his wife began a private fast which continued for about one week. People began coming into their home praying through to the Holy Spirit. Some even drove from out of town for this special God-sent revival. Soon thereafter, a district meeting of the churches convened at his church and a number of people noted the power-packed services. This special powerful presence of the Lord continued in the church for weeks after this.

Another minister told of his very first revival, which was conducted in a country schoolhouse. He and others agreed to fast and pray for three days and nights. The revival continued with good attendance for seven weeks. Every night people were at the altar praying through to "old-time salvation."

One man of God told of a mighty move of God in revival following weeks of prayer and fasting by his local congregation. The crowds became so great that extra seating had to be prepared and parking became a problem. There were ninety salvation experiences in this outpouring of the divine presence.

The same man related a similar event in which a oweek revival was planned. But God so moved that the meeting was extended to three weeks.

A pastor described a wonderful experience in fasting at a time when he worked in the coal mines of Kentucky. He worked the coal mines by day and preached every night of a three-week revival. He fasted ten days of the revival asking the Lord for thirty souls. At the end of his fast on a Sunday morning, he went into the woods to pray.

Before he left the house, the Lord showed him the place he was to pray: there he would find a log, a certain rock, and a sunken place. The Spirit of God directed him until he found the designated place. After he prayed, as he rose to leave, all around him the bushes were covered with beautiful white flowers. He thought he would pick his wife a bouquet, but the Lord told him not to touch them. Then he realized that this was a most glorious vision. He has been to this place a number of times since and there have never been flowers on those same bushes. That very Sunday night fifty-three sinners came to the altar with thirty of them receiving salvation. At the end of the three weeks twenty-five were added to the church.

Miracles of Healing

By far the longest list of fasting results is that of physical and mental healing. A businessman recollected the habit of his minister father to fast one meal a day for more than thirty years. The motives for his constant practice were personal discipline and to give the money saved to the missions. He quickly recalled a very painful toothache he had as a boy. His father laid his hand on his cheek as he prayed. The pain instantly left and he fell asleep before his father finished his prayer. This same young man witnessed a cancer on his mother's lip fall off. In later years his fasting father lay critically ill, vomiting day and night for two weeks. It appeared he would die, but he suddenly was healed.

In 1951 a minister was stricken with inflammatory rheumatism for six weeks. Friends fasted and prayed until God intervened. Another minister's daughter developed pneumonia. The parents were desperate for help. After a few days of fasting and praying, the child was dramatically and instantaneously healed.

A man and a woman were healed of bleeding ulcers following fasts. In the first case the man had been plagued with the sickness for fifteen years, living on bland foods the entire time. The previous four to five years he had hemorrhaged quite often. At times he grew extremely weak and thought he would not live. He decided to fast for his condition. Not until the seventh day did he drink a small amount of orange juice. On the eighth day he ate two eggs, two pieces of pork sausage and biscuits. That night for supper he ate pinto beans with pork hocks, onion, and cornbread. His stomach has not hurt or heamorrohaged since that time. The Lord completely healed him.

In the second ulcer case, a family member called a fast. She wrote to eight brothers and sisters asking them to set aside one particular day for fasting and prayer for their sister. Following the fast the sister grew worse, but she determined to trust God. Enduring much pain, she rested propped up on a sofa. She and her daughter prayed three days and nights. She called her pastor and his wife to pray. The pastor declared her healed on the authority of God's Word. He told her to eat whatever she wanted. She asked for an egg and bacon. A doctor had diagnosed her condition, which had persisted for two years, as bleeding ulcers. At this report she has taken no medication and has eaten anything she wants without pain for about two months.

A dear friend wrote of a terrible accident and subsequent miracle of healing he witnessed several years ago. He was terrified while he helplessly watched the brakes fail on a heavy earthmover. The machine gained momentum as it traveled down a steep hill. The operator tried but was unable to stop or slow it by digging the blade into the ground. Some children were dangerously near its path. In desperation the driver turned sharply to the left. The machine overturned, pinning him beneath. He appeared dead as he was dragged from beneath the earthmover. While an ambulance was summoned, efforts were made to resuscitate him. Shortly before the ambulance arrived, he began to breathe and groan.

He was rushed to the hospital bleeding from his mouth, nose, and ears. His face was turning dark and his neck was swelling rapidly. The attending physician gave no hope for his recovery. X-rays revealed three crushed vertabrae, all the ribs on the left side broken, a punctured lung, and other internal injuries.

In the meantime phones were ringing and concerned people immediately began fasting and praying. The doctor told the eyewitnesses that the man could not live through the night. However, the next morning the doctor found the injured man alive and conscious. The surprised doctor exclaimed, "Surely, the Man upstairs was with you last night."

The pressure of the heavy machine had caused the blood to almost exude from the skin of his face and neck. Even his eyeballs were so extremely bloodshot that he could not see. However, the church continued fasting and praying, and he miraculously began to improve. The doctors determined that he would spend months immobile in cumbersome braces. In spite of all this, the injured man was out of the hospital in less than three weeks. He travelled seven hundred miles to give his testimony to thousands of people gathered for an annual assembly. He fully recovered and became physically active in a short time with no apparent serious side effects.

This same minister friend also wrote of another healing. A deacon's wife who had become ill and lost much weight was taken to the hospital for tests. The diagnosis was malignancy of the stomach in a very advanced stage. The doctors agreed she would not live more than a few days at the very most. She decided she would rather spend her last days at home. The doctors granted permission for her discharge with the warning that the move could hasten her death.

Upon her arrival home, the pastor was called for prayer and counseling. He read some Scriptures, anointed her with oil, and fervently prayed. The Bible was left open on a small table at her bedside to James 5:14-16.

The local congregation was called to prayer and lasting. For quite some time she remained in critical condition, but eventually she began to eat and regain strength. She progressively gained weight and strength and was soon able to resume caring for her husband and three daughters.

Six months later she and her husband returned to the hospital. The doctors recognized her husband by name. He asked them if they knew the lady with him. They did not recognize her. When he finally convinced them that she was the same woman whom they had given up to die, they declared it was indeed a miracle of God. She lived some forty years afterwards as a living witness of the divine power of God in response to a fasting, praying people.

A dear fasting, praying couple told of their first fast several years ago. Their oldest daughter was mentally handicapped from birth. She was unable to learn and remained in the first grade for three years, enduring teasing because of her size. The parents were desperate for help. They had no knowledge of people praying for healing until a preacher came for a revival in their neighborhood. He believed God would help the girl, so he asked the neighbors to fast three days in earnest prayer. The mother wrote that they lived on a farm at the time, and that in the midst of the summer's heat and the fast she had to clean out the brooder house. At such times she had always stopped several times for a drink of water, but she marvelled at how God strengthened her without water.

About two weeks after the fast, the school teacher asked the child's father what had happened. There was a tremendous change and she was learning as she should for the first time. I personally know of this child and can verify that she is able to read and write better than some adults without a mental handicap.

Another testimony of divine healing resulting from fasting and prayer occurred in 1962. A lady was hospitalized in Goiania, Goias, Brazil for the second time in three months with pancreatitis. She had been unable to eat for more than two weeks; the smell of food or drink made her deathly ill. The doctors were baffled at her failure to respond favorably to their treatments.

As she grew weaker, the doctors scheduled exploratory surgery for the following Monday. Fearing that she would not live through surgery, they encouraged her to write to anyone she wished and leave the letters with them. If she lived, they would return the unmailed letters. If she died, they would mail them.

Without her knowing about it, on the Saturday prior to the scheduled surgery, a group of Brazilian Christians in the little town of Goiandira, about one hundred miles away, felt that they should fast and pray for her healing. That Saturday they fasted breakfast and prayed. Continuing to pray into the morning they felt before noon that the Lord had answered their prayers. They believed she would recover and that it was unnecessary to continue their fast. They ate lunch as usual and went about their regular duties. Because there was no telephone service in that area, she did not learn about their praying and fasting until several days later.

The very morning this group of people prayed for her, the presence of God entered the hospital room and wonderfully healed her. She sensed it. That afternoon she ate a boiled potato with no seasoning. This was the first food she had eaten for many days. Surgery was not necessary. A few days later she was released from the hospital and has never been a hospital patient since that time. She felt that the Lord literally gave her back her life and she determined to live the rest of it out for His glory.

Miracles of Salvation

The sixth category is miracles of salvation. Although every person who comes face to face with God and is cleansed by the precious blood of Jesus Christ His Son experiences a miracle of God's love and grace, there are some whose conversion seems more miraculous.

One such example is that of a businessman who had a fasting, praying father. He told me of how he was in an airplane. There was no church around. There were no Christians to speak with him about his soul or pray with him. Suddenly, as he sat there, a tremendous convicting presence seized him. Within a few minutes he had surrendered his life to the Lord. He has been a faithful servant of his Savior since that day.

A college instructor wrote of how her mother prayed many years for a wayward son. Early in 1983 her mother began to fast and pray for him. She was eighty-five years old at the time. The Lord gave her peace, and she said, "He is going to be saved; the Lord told me so."

Shortly thereafter, she entered the hospital. The surgeon decided to schedule surgery for the next morning. Before the surgeon's decision was known, the son, who lived in another state, called to tell his mother that he had received Christ into his heart. It was a glorious confirmation to her of the word she had received from the Lord during her earlier season of fasting and prayer. This episode is especially precious to this family since their mother did not recover from the surgery.

A Pentecostal minister related an unusual incident of salvation to me in which the overseer of his area asked all the churches to join in a continuous forty-eight-hour fast. The people took their toothbrushes and washcloths with them to the church at midnight on Thursday and stayed until midnight on Saturday. This was a constant vigil without food or drink. Prayer was made every hour on the hour. Bible studies, devotions, messages and testimonies were given. During the night especially, great outpourings of the Holy Spirit were experienced which seemed to take the people into a different dimension. He stated that there was weakness of the body, the knees and limbs, and dryness of the throat, but as soon as the people became involved in the worship, these symptoms disappeared.

At about ten o'clock on the last night, the pastor of the church was so weak that he quietly said to the Lord, "I have run out of things to do and have no strength to do more." At that time his eyes rested on a young man who was not a Christian, but had sung before in the services. The pastor asked him to sing. As he sang, the Holy Spirit convicted him of his sin and he tried to cut the song short to return to his seat. The pastor stopped him and said, "You're three feet from the altar, turn around and accept Jesus." He hesitated, then stepped to the altar to pray. As through an opened valve, the power of the Holy Spirit flooded the place and in seconds the altar was filled with curious onlookers. In the next hour and a half, seven were saved, including a young man for whom the church had prayed for over ten years. The next morning, at the end of Sunday School, there was such a strong convicting power present that the superintendent gave an invitation and twelve were saved without any preaching. In the regular services during that week there were thirty-six such experiences in succession with eight joining the church.

A retired minister told of another powerful act of conviction and salvation upon a young man from the Blue Ridge Mountains of Virginia in the early part of 1930. There was a mighty revival in progress with people praying through each night. Many young people attended the revival. Some were interested, but others were there only to make fun of the people. Among this latter group was a young man whom the pastor's daughter had seemed to fall in love with at first sight. The father would not allow her to date him unless he gave his heart to the Lord. The devout Christian girl was in love with him, and remembering that Christians were not to be unequally yoked together with unbelievers (2 Cor. 6:14 KJV), she began to fast and pray for his salvation.

On the ninth day of her fast the powers of Satan were broken and the young man fell down at the altar where he prayed through to the gift of the Holy Spirit. The next year this couple was married. Later he was called into the ministry and served as pastor, district overseer, and state overseer. God blessed this union with several children who are ministers of the gospel.

Within the last few years a mother became especially burdened for her youngest son. She felt the grip of Satan upon him and felt if he were not saved that summer, he would be eternally lost. This woman began fasting and praying for his salvation. On the fifth night of her fast, between two and three o'clock in the morning, Proverbs 29:1 was impressed in her mind. The words came to her forcefully, "He, that being often reproved hardeneth his neck, shall suddenly be destroyed, and that without remedy.

She was compelled in her spirit to call her son, who was in another state on vacation with relatives, to quote him the verse. Soon thereafter, he accompanied several family members to a river. They were walking along on a sandbar when it fell into a whirlpool of water. The water sucked them helplessly down until it appeared all would go under. Her son tried to save one of the children, but in his own desperate struggle he went under again and again. Blackness closed in on him. He knew he would drown. In an instant he remembered the words of a Sunday school teacher. The teacher warned that if the young man would not give his life to God, God would not let him have his life. He remembered his mother's Scripture and called to God to save him. About that time what appeared to be a big log came up under him and carried him the shore, where he vomited blood and muddy water. However, none of the witnesses ever saw the log. God had miraculously saved his life. In turn he gave it to the one who saved him.

The final narrative of miraculous salvation concerns a man who had been raised in a Christian home by sincere, praying parents. Although he attended church regularly, he showed no intention of committing his life to the Lord. He eventually married a Christian girl who joined his parents in prayer for his salvation, but apparently to no avail.

In a four-week revival God moved mightily upon Christians with soul burdens. Many were being converted because of heavy conviction. This young man's mother became so burdened for him that she could not eat and could scarcely sleep. She would weep and moan by the hour. At times she seemed oblivious to life about her. She seemed in a trance in her agony. In her fasting and deep distress she began to weaken physically.

Her son seemed untouched until others began to fear she would die. Finally, he was struck with conviction. He became so overcome with conviction that it seemed he would die. He had to be helped into the church for services. His facial features resembled one condemned to death. Although he groaned at the altar in his distress, he could not pray. Finally, after some time, he was able to express his sorrow to God for his sins, and was forgiven. His countenance changed; his callousness was gone. He had surrendered his life to the Lord, because of a fasting, praying mother who dared to challenge Susan's claim on the soul of her son. Through Christ, Satan was defeated and salvation was won.

In two other cases I have on hand, backsliders surrendered to the Lord following pastoral fasts. One pastor had fasted ten days when he and his wife went to pray for a backslider. She and her husband both prayed through to victory. The other pastor had fasted a week when an erring member repented.

I have two reports of people fasting to receive the Holy Spirit. One teenager fasted one day, passing up his favorite chicken dinner which his mother had prepared. That very night be received the Holy Spirit. Prior to this night, he had prayed and prayed, but could not claim this precious gift.

Church Problems Solved

One pastor reported a serious problem in his congregation that was sure to destroy the progress of the church. The pastor's wife was impressed to fast. After three days of fasting and prayer, God gave the pastor's family special grace and wisdom to deal with the serious situation.

Another pastor told of a very strange problem which arose in his rather large congregation. In every service, before the devotional was finished, a binding spirit would so hinder the congregation that they could hardly sing, pray, or testify. The pastor and even visiting ministers could not preach. The sermons were always a failure. As long as the pastor was away from the church, he could pray victoriously, but when he returned to the church the same spirit confronted him. Ultimately, the pastor and his congregation felt they could not go on in such a state.

One Sunday morning the pastor's text was taken from Matthew 18:19, "Again I say unto you, that if two of you shall agree on earth as touching any thing they shall ask, it shall be done for them of my Father which is in heaven." An invitation was given for those to come forward who would agree with the pastor to fast and pray until victory came. Nine came forward.

Everything continued as usual until the end of the week. On Saturday night the pastor was at the church preparing his Sunday morning sermon when a car swung into the front parking area. The young man who emerged was in such a great rush that he did not turn off his lights or close his door. He rushed into the church crying so loud and hard that the pastor could scarcely understand his problem. Finally, he realized that the young member was confessing an ongoing sexual relationship with a young lady who was also a member of the church. After the two made appropriate confession, the hindering spirit left the church. God had not been pleased with habitual sin in the church and had withdrawn their freedom in the

Spirit. When concerned individuals united in a fasting effort, the power of the enemy was broken.

This pastor also remembered in one of his congregations a very quiet lady who always knew when he was in a severe trial. She would call and ask the pastor if she could join in fasting and praying about the matter. She would never allow him to tell her about the problem. She felt it was none of her business. God knew about it and that was what was important. As soon as she took this burden upon herself in prayer and fasting answers soon came. It never failed.

Years later, after this pastor had moved on, he inquired of subsequent pastors about the burden-bearing lady. They confirmed the same sharing of burdens and the same victorious results. One of the later pastors grew very discouraged in his pastoral ministry there and had secretly packed his belongings to move when she called asking his permission to pray and fast for him. As a result of her prayers and fasting, the pastor unpacked and remained until the Lord was finished with him in that place.

One state overseer began to observe a leanness of soul and a coolness of the affections toward God in his state. He proclaimed a fast day on Tuesday of every week for several months. There was a marked change in the spirituality of his ministers and in church growth.

Whatever the problem, whether a hindering spirit, a severe trial, leanness of soul, or another serious problem, prayer and fasting is attested in these accounts as effective.

Divine Wisdom and Direction

I have mentioned in earlier accounts how wisdom to give answers for problems superseded all ability prior to the fasting experience. But there is one especially interesting act of divine guidance that I want to share here.

A Georgia pastor felt impressed to plant a church in a nearby town. He habitually fasted. As he and four or five other Christian men traveled toward the town, they stopped to pray in a wooded area for divine direction for a place in which to have a service. While praying, the pastor had a vision of a house where they were to have the evening service. Not having had this type of experience before, he agreed with the others that they would drive up and down the streets of the town until the Holy Spirit spontaneously witnessed through them all. When the Holy Spirit manifested himself at once through them, the pastor looked around to see the house of his vision.

When they went to the door of the home an invalid lady called for them to come in. She very much wanted to have a meeting in her home. Also, in another part of the same house a young couple desired Christian fellowship and worship. In addition to this, the men went to stay in a hotel whose owner gave them free food and lodging while they were having their meetings. He even opened two of his places of business for services.

Acts of Divine Judgment

A young Christian man who had a very fine prosperous job related this story. He loved his job, but his boss was extremely oppressive. He constantly criticized and tore apart project plans that had taken long periods of time to prepare. They had to be replanned and prepared again. The young man could hardly bear the torment. One day he asked a fellow Christian employee to fast and pray about this matter. At the end of a three-day fast, the boss had a heart attack and died. A very cordial, encouraging man took his place.

An evangelist was called for a revival in a western city. The church had been trying to establish a congregation there, but every attempt seemed fruitless. This evangelist had been fasting and praying prior to the revival, but still their labor seemed in vain. One night, in the midst of the meeting, two men burst through the front door of the church. One was chasing the other with a knife. An usher stationed near the door grabbed the knife-wielding man and threw him to the floor, taking the knife. The man was so furious that he began to rave and curse. The evangelist informed him that this was a place of worship and he was not to talk like that. The angry man threatened the life of the evangelist and left, promising to return for him. The evangelist called the worshipers to prayer. Not long afterward they heard a loud commotion outside the church. The knife-wielding man had been hit by a car while running across the street. He was believed to have been killed outright. Fear gripped the congregation and a revival broke out; twenty-one were baptized in water and seventeen were added to the church.

It must be observed here that in neither case did anyone at any time fast and pray that their enemies would die. However, in God's sovereignty they were removed. These are fearful accounts, but God will always protect and care for His own. These accounts are reminiscent of the fast of Queen Esther and her people. After fasting three days and nights, the man who planned to destroy the Jews was hanged on his own gallows.

Supernatural Visitations

I have previously mentioned in this chapter the divine presence, several visions, and a visiting angel. Another man told of the sensation of an angel visiting his room. He said that this experience was vivid for days. He also had a vision of Christ healing blind Bartimaeus. For years afterward, he received exceptional anointing and outstanding results when he preached about this healing.

A lady who fasts regularly experienced a wonderful dream about twenty-five years ago. She saw the most beautiful crystal-clear stream. Across it was an arched stone footbridge and the brightest colored flowers banked on the other side of the stream. A lush green meadow was stretched beyond the stream as far as the eye could see. She recognized it as a glimpse of heaven. From time to time the scene returned to comfort and sustain her.

Then in 1980 this place of indescribable beauty appeared in a vision with one change. Jesus, like a gentle shepherd, was strolling along the green meadow. The sight of Him brought an even greater peace and comfort. It was at this very time she learned that her mother, who lived hundreds of miles away, was terminally ill with cancer. But this vision strengthened the daughter throughout the coming months.

In the same hour of her mother's death, she stood exhausted and grieved at the foot of her bed. Suddenly the vision came to her mind and she turned to share it with an uncle. Just then her mother began drawing her last breath so that the story was never told.

The next few days were difficult and busy preparing for the funeral. The vision was forgotten. But in the midst of the funeral, while she sat listening to the service, the vision vividly returned. This time, in addition to seeing Jesus robed in white walking along in an emerald green meadow, there was another figure. It was her mother walking hand in hand with her Savior. She had the most radiant countenance, which was an expression of her joy and contentment to be home at last. This was such a heavenly experience to the daughter that she has continued to draw solace from it to this time. In fact, it was such a sacred event, she has scarcely spoken of it until this writing. It was so real that it still brings tears of gladness and appreciation for a Heavenly Father who ministered to her in this unusual way.

CHAPTER 16

THE PRACTICAL ASPECTS OF FASTING

In order to provide you with an ample guide for fasting, it is necessary to speak of some practical aspects of fasting, and also of some possible negative aspects. The negative aspects are exceptions in fasting experiences and not to be feared as common. The purpose in addressing these possibilities in a practical way is to warn and prepare you for the devices of Satan so that you will be well-prepared.

Fasting people have observed that one may be more sensitive to both spirit worlds. While one is more sensitive to the Spirit of God, he may also be more sensitive to the spirit of Satan. Recalling the forty-day fast of Jesus, we note that He was tempted in three areas: the lust of the flesh, the lust of the eyes, and the pride of life. Likewise, some of our peers speak of similar temptations.

Recall the young minister mentioned earlier, who battled with the lust of the flesh. Another friend turned his radio on to listen to the news during a time of fasting. Prior to the news, a country song about gambling was playing. The lyrics of the song stuck in his mind and he fought a terrible battle to rid his mind of them so that he could again turn his attention to God in meditation. The victory came when he quoted this appropriate Scripture against the enemy, "Let the words of my mouth, and the meditation of my heart, be acceptable in thy sight, O Lord, my strength, and my redeemer (Ps. 19:14).

This same friend told of the temptation to eat, thus breaking his fast. He had read that by the third or fourth day, one was usually not so hungry and tempted by food. However, he continued on for days being tempted by visions of food. On the sixth day he got out his wife's cookbooks. He read outloud recipe after recipe and remarked to his wife how delicious they sounded. He prepared the family meals. Finally, victory came. He had won the battle by confronting the devil with his own weapon. This is not unscriptural. Again, remembering the temptation of Jesus, the weapon of Satan was Scripture. Jesus overcame the temptation with Scripture.

Finally one may be tempted to self-righteousness, Satan may plant in one's mind thoughts of being closer to God than non-fasters. Or he may plant thoughts of God's indebtedness for the extraordinary sacrifices of fasting. These may be the enemy's favorite devices. If he succeeds, he can stop the blessings of God by blocking communication.

By trial and error some have discovered several useful and wise practical helps. Most fasters recommend eating lightly beginning a few days before the fast. One eats lightly on the third day before the fast. On the second day before he eats all the fresh fruit he wants but only fruit. On the final day before the fast he drinks only fruit juices. He also recommends coming out of the fast in a similar manner. This causes loss stomach distress. He adds that it is best to drink only distilled wirer during the fast. Regular tap water may cause stomach problems.

Some choose to separate themselves from their spouse and even from the world at large while fasting. Others are unable to do this. One may do as he prefers in this matter. However, it is scriptural to have the approval of one's companion before separating from him for the fast (1 Cor. 7:5).

For further practical encouragement I have chosen two daily journals to share with you. Each of them covers ten days. The first belongs to a minister's wife; the second belongs to a minister.

Monday: I awoke feeling the need to go on a fast. I ate lightly today—french toast for breakfast, hamburger and fries for lunch; and soup and sandwich for supper.

Tuesday: I drank fruit juices today. I ate cheese and crackers for lunch and fruit salad for supper. I am hungry and have a headache.

Wednesday: This was the first day of the fast. I had a headache and was nauseated all day. I vomited at night so I didn't get to attend church.

Thursday (second day): I'm feeling better today, just very weak. I craved food. I sang in a revival with more anointing than I've experienced in a while.

Friday (third day): I had to go to Nashville to the hospital with my husband. I felt very weak this morning, but stronger as the day passed. I had an intense craving for food. I've lost about six pounds.

Saturday (fourth day): I felt weak this morning, but strength increased. Workers remodeled the bathroom all day and I prepared supper for them. I had a desire for food, but no craving. I worked two hours cleaning the church and the rest of the day cleaning at home. I had average strength.

Sunday (fifth day): I felt good physically. I prepared dinner for my family without temptation. I had a few slight weak spells in church. Friends came after church and brought pizza. I was really tempted.

Monday (sixth day): I have lost nine or ten pounds. Last night and tonight I drank cups of warm water. It tasted good. I was very weak this morning, but my strength increased and I bought groceries and cooked supper for my family. I really desire food, but am having no trouble passing it up.

Tuesday (seventh day): I'm extremely weak today. I cooked supper without much desire. Tonight I developed a sore throat and had some dizzy spells. Thank God for His help and strength I can't remember which night, but one night recently I was awakened with a friend on my mind and felt a real need to pray. My sleep is not normal. I am sleeping light and waking up a lot.

Wednesday (eighth day): Today was a bad day physically. I woke up with a cold and was weak all day, but I had no desire for food. I cooked supper and did my housework. I also planned and moderated the youth service.

Thursday (ninth day): I cooked supper and ran errands. I'm weak, but have no desire for food.

Friday (tenth day): My mother and my nephew came today for Easter weekend. I worked very hard preparing for them. I have more strength today and I cooked supper.

Saturday: I drank juices all day. I ate salad for supper. It tasted wonderful.

Sunday: I had Easter dinner at church and ate normal, but tonight I had diahrrea. I'm sure I ate too soon. I should have come off the fast more gradually. However, it wasn't too bad.

Although I lost about eighteen pounds on the fast, I gained most of it back. After the fast, I craved food and ate more than usual. I didn't feel any different spiritually, but the Lord answered some personal needs for me later. They were battles I had been fighting in my mind. The fast seemed to be a sacrifice showing the Lord my great love for Him. Since the fast, I have had a greater desire for deeper fellowship with Him. I would like to go on another fast when my schedule is not so demanding. I am really feeling the need for a slowing down of my lifestyle and having more active communion with the Lord.

I later learned that the friend I was awakened to pray for was going through a great trial, but made it through victoriously. That gave me greater incentive to follow the Lord's leadings.

During the fast, I felt that I was so short with my family. I was easily irritated. This was a hindrance from Satan. Considering the temptations to anger and the physical weakness, the fast was very worthwhile. It was the beginning of a much deeper relationship with the Lord. My husband noticed the change.

She added some brief notes from another ten-day fast about one year later. She and her husband were changing pastorates. They were overwhelmed with their new responsibility so the two of them fasted together for ten days. In this fast she did not experience the pain, discomfort, or cravings of her earlier fast. In fact, none of these occurred. She prepared food for her son and company with no temptation or desire for it. God gave her Psalm 71:16, "I will go in the strength of the Lord God." This was the source of her strength.

Several months later she noted what a difficult period of adjustment and time of tremendous change it had been for her. She said, "I'm learning and the Lord is teaching me that true satisfaction is only found in Him and His will." However, if it had not been for the fast and the definite answer about their ministry, she would have gone under. Through all of this she developed a deeper relationship with the Lord. She can better handle stress. She believes the Lord is working some greater thing for her.

The minister's journal of his ten-day fast is as follows:

First day: For some time now I have been compelled to follow the Lord in an extended consecration fast. Today I am battling whether to begin now or wait until the pressure is less and my schedule slows some. After another prayer, the decision has been reached. Now is the time.

I shared my thoughts and plans with my wife to which she agreed. Lunch is my last meal. (Homemade grilled hamburgers, etc. is not ideal for the pre-fast, but they are my favorites.) There are so many demands and no time to fast.

But I have to. It's important. I'm really having a hard time with my mind in trying to reach a decision to start today.

After another prayer, my mind is made up. There will be no better time than now. This is a big part of the battle—making up my mind. Before bedtime I already had hunger pangs. I feel like I could eat almost anything. The devil tried to throw the praying fasting child of God off course. James 4:7, 8 really works. If I submit myself to God and resist the devil, he will flee from me. If I draw nigh to God, He will draw nigh to me.

Some members of my family are visiting. This means socializing, eating, and going. They had already planned to visit us before this time of fasting. My wife prepared a nice meal. I excused myself while they ate. They went on with their activities while I spent the evening in prayer and communion with the Lord. We, the Lord and I, had a wonderful evening. I was hungry and tempted to eat, but God gave a made-up mind.

This has been a good day. My schedule of ministerial activities was nearly normal. I spent a few hours in the office, visited some folks, and ran errands. I had a good evening at home retiring early. I'm not much interested in reading (the Bible is my only reading material during the fast). My eyes are a little tired, but I have no headache. Praise the Lord!

Second day: I've spent most of today in prayer and Bible reading. His presence was near. This morning was fairly normal. I was at the office some. In the evening I attended a mid-week service.

Fasting time seems like time wasted, especially the first few days starting. Today is dull. I am hungry and weak. I have no spirit to pray. However, I am aware of the devil's tricks. I know I am really making more progress than he would have me think. Oh, but the Lord is so real.

I restate the purpose of this fast. It is for personal consecration. I am not trying to change the mind of God to please me. Rather, I want to find His will. I desire to be changed into His likeness and be able to say, "Yes, Lord." I want to be genuine with no guile. I desire to be a clean vessel, useful to Him. Maybe I've been trying to tell the Lord what I need and when I need it. Now I am changing my prayer to say, "Lord, show me the way."

Third day: I have no headache or other body discomforts. I'm tempted with food thoughts. I'm drinking purified water at room temperature. But it doesn't taste good. I am packing the car for a trip. I'm glad my wife will drive.

After several hours of travel, I settled into a motel room for a few days. My wife is in a meeting a short distance away. In prayer I was trying to encourage the Lord to be with me. I need Him. Then He spoke to me. He said, "I have already told you I will never leave you or forsake you." What a wonderful reminder. It was so encouraging.

Fourth day: This is my best day so far. My strength is better than the past three days. The bothersome thoughts of food have diminished. I have no headache or other physical problems. My prayers and communion are more finely tuned to the Lord. Psalm 104 reminded me of how big and wonderful God is. I was deeply impressed with this chapter this morning. I have been meditating on it today. All the

Scripture jumps out at me when I'm reading. It seems I could preach on nearly any verse. It's such a good feeling.

Fifth day: After a devotion, I went walking with the Lord. I'm doing fine. I have no headache or other problem. I'm a little slower, but in good physical condition and in a precious frame of mind. It is simply wonderful not to be taunted with trivial worldly thoughts, ideas, and suggestions. I've noticed the past couple of days that all my senses are keener than usual.

Spiritually, I am on the victory side. I didn't have time in my schedule to fast now, but I am. I have victory over a pressing schedule. I have victory over food and victory over my appetite. It is true that prayer is intensified with fasting. My praying has not been loud or long. But what precious communion with the Lord.

Yesterday (fourth day) it seemed that I was simply lifted above the shadows of this world. I was free from the mental anguish of worldly temptation. There is a whole new world of excitement in the exquisite presence of the Lord when one is lifted above the shadows, when one mounts above the clouds! Praise the name of the Lord!

Sixth day: Today is Sunday. I slept none last night. I had no problem. I just was not sleepy. I stayed busy meditating on the Lord, praying thinking, and reading the Word. I'm feeling fine today.

I decided to drop in on the Sunday morning service of our local church in the area. Without preparation, I was called on to preach. I felt some physical weakness and thought of just sharing a Scripture; however, the Spirit of the Lord gave me n special anointing for more than an hour. How wonderful is the inspiration that results from being in tune with the Lord. (The pastor did not know I was fasting.)

This afternoon my wife and I returned home. I'm a little weak, but the Lord is so near. There's no battle now. Food temptations are gone. Victory is mine. Thank the Lord. Now there is not so much impatience. I'm just having a wonderful time basking in the spiritual sunlight of His presence.

Seventh day: I'm feeling wonderful in spirit and body. I was busy with a fairly full schedule of normal activities. I am a little weak at times and move a little more slowly. But I have no problems. His presence seems so much clearer and nearer.

Eighth day: I had a normal day of activities at home and the office. I visited one in the hospital. I am having a difficult time encouraging my wife to eat. She is too sympathetic. Food is not a problem. However, throughout this fast, there is a conquering of the flesh. There is a sense of glorious victory. I have spent much time reading the Word and praying.

Ninth day: I had almost a full day of normal activity. I was a little weak physically, but am strong in spirit. It is impossible to describe the many benefits these days of fasting have wrought. There is a genuine awareness that God is Jehovah, infinitely and eternally, and I am less than nothing. I pray, "Lord, let me find you, your will, your timing, your directive, and the grace to obey."

Tenth day: Although I am nearly a half-century old, them have been no physical difficulties except some weakness. My digestive tract and stomach feel fine. These ten days have caused me to lose about sixteen pounds. But I do not mind because there is a special nearness of Him. There was no crisis or problem pressing me into this fast. Just a challenge of the Lord to draw closer to Him.

Finally he shares two important insights. The time of breaking the fast is of extreme importance. This time seems to require more resolve, discipline, and determination than any time throughout the entire ten days. Restraint from too much food and activity is necessary for a few days.

He has also learned that rather than leaving an extended fast to go zooming upward with great victory, the opposite is true. However, after a little time of drifting through a valley, victory comes. "I have greater anointing for the service of the Lord. My nerves are more relaxed in important business decisions. I have a keener perspective with the Lord. To Him be glory and honor and dominion and power, both now and forever!"

No two journals will read alike of course. Each will have its own story, for they are as unique as the penman who writes them. However, these are valuable so that we may compare them with our own experiences or to provide guidelines for our own fasts.

Many of the powerful personal fasting testimonies quoted in the last chapter date back about fifty years to the days of old-time Holy Ghost revival. Fasting and praying was the impetus for all these numerous unusual occurrences. These are not the conclusions of one person from this period, but of several witnesses of integrity who have come forward to affirm their fasting experiences. Were it not for the integrity of those whom I have interviewed, I would have been skeptical of the phenomena they have confirmed. However, God who changes not is still at work for those who will turn their full attention upon Him.

The examples of these contemporary spiritual leaders beckon us to follow suit. This is the very answer to our twentieth-century dilemma. We cannot argue that it is not effective. Here stands ample testimony to the fact. The half has not been told. I had only a few short weeks to collect these declarations. I believe volumes could be written if time and opportunity permitted all who know of such examples to come forward.

Even at this moment there is an undercurrent of dedicated people who are quietly paying the price of self-discipline and focusing their full attention upon a God who is rewarding. I know of a large church whose congregation is in a forty-day fast as I write this. At least one member is fasting daily for this period of time. Recently, ninety people in one state fasted ten days each. People are hungry for God and answers to prayer. God through fasting and prayer is responding to the cries of His people.

APPENDIX A

The following is an edited resolution taken from the *Journals of the House of Burgesses of Virginia, 1773-1776:*

Tuesday, the 24th of May, 14 Geo. III. 1774

This House, being deeply impressed with Apprehension of the great Dangers, to be derived to British America, from the hostile Invasion of the City of Boston, in our Sister Colony of Massachusetts Bay, whose Commerce and Harbour are, on the first Day of June next, to be stopped by an armed Force, deem it highly necessary that the said first Day of June be set apart, by the Members of this House, as a Day of Fasting, Humiliation, and Prayer, devoutly to implore the Divine Interposition, for averting the heavy Calamity which threatens Destruction to our civil Rights, and the Evils of civil War; to give us one Heart and one Mind to oppose, by all just and proper Means, every Injury to American Rights . . . .

Ordered, therefore, that the Members of this House do attend in their Places, at the Hour of ten in the Forenoon, on the said first Day of June next, in order to proceed with the Speaker, and the Mace, to the Church in this City, for the Purposes aforesaid; and that the Reverend Mr. Price be appointed to read Prayers, and the Reverend Mr. Gwatkin, to preach a Sermon, suitable to the Occasion.

Appendix B

By the President of the United States of America.

A PROCLAMATION.

As the safety and prosperity of nations ultimately and essentially depend on the protection and the blessing of Almighty God, and the national acknowledgment of this truth is not only an indispensable duty which the people owe to Him, but a duty whose natural influence is favorable to the promotion of that morality and piety without which social happiness can not exist nor the blessings of a free government be enjoyed; and as this duty, at all times incumbent, is so especially in seasons of difficulty or of danger, when existing or threatening calamities, the just judgements of God against prevalent iniquity, are a loud call to repentance and reformation; and as the United States of America are at present placed in a hazardous and afflictive situation by the unfriendly disposition, conduct, and demands of a foreign power, evinced by repeated refusals to receive our messengers of reconciliation and peace, by depredations on our commerce, and the infliction of injuries on very many of our fellow-citizens while engaged in their lawful business on the seas—under these considerations it has appeared to me that the duty of imploring the mercy and benediction of Heaven on our country demands at this time a special attention from its inhabitants.

I have therefore thought fit to recommend, and I do hereby recommend, that Wednesday, the 9th day of May next, be observed throughout the United States as a day of solemn humiliation, fasting, and prayer; that the citizens of these States, abstaining on that day from their customary worldly occupations, offer their devout addresses to the Father of Mercies agreeably to those forms or methods which they have severally adopted as the most suitable and becoming; that all religious congregations do, with the deepest humility, acknowledge before God the manifold sins and transgressions with which we are justly chargeable as individuals and as a nation, beseeching Him at the same time, of His infinite grace, through the Redeemer of the World, freely to remit all our offenses, and to incline us by His Holy Spirit to that sincere repentance and reformation which may afford us reason to hope for his inestimable favor and heavenly benediction; that it be made the subject of particular and earnest supplication that our country may be protected from all the dangers which threaten it; that our civil and religious privileges may be preserved inviolate and perpetuated to the latest generations; that our public councils and magistrates may be especially enlightened and directed at this critical period; that the American people may be united in those bonds of amity and mutual confidence and inspired with that vigor and fortitude by which they have in times past been so highly distinguished and by which they have obtained such invaluable advantages; that the health of the inhabitants of our land may be preserved, and their agriculture, commerce, fisheries, arts, and manufacturers be blessed and prospered; that the principles of genuine piety and sound morality may influence the minds and govern the lives of every description of our citizens, and that the blessings of peace, freedom, and pure religion may be speedily extended to all the nations of the earth.

And finally, I recommend that on the said day the duties of humiliation and prayer be accompanied by fervent thanksgiving to the Bestower of Every Good Gift, not only for His having hitherto protected and preserved the people of these United States in the independent enjoyment of their religious and civil freedom, but also for having prospered them in a wonderful progress of population, and for conferring on them many and great favors conducive to the happiness and prosperity of a nation.

Given under my hand and the seal of the United States of America, at Philadelphia, this 23rd day of March, A.D. 1798, and of the independence of the said States the twenty-second.

JOHN ADAMS.

By the President:
TIMOTHY PICKERING,
Secretary of State.[2]

APPENDIX C

By the President of the United States of America.

A PROCLAMATION.

The two Houses of the National Legislature having by a joint resolution expressed their desire that in the present time of public calamity and war a day may be recommended to be observed by the people of the United States as a day of public humiliation and fasting and of prayer to Almighty God for the safety and welfare of these States, His blessing on their arms, and a speedy restoration of peace, I have deemed it proper by this proclamation to recommend that Thursday, the 12th of January next, be set apart as a day of which all may have an opportunity of voluntarily offering at the same time in their respective religious assemblies their humble adoration to the Great Sovereign of the Universe, of confessing their sins and transgressions, and of strengthening their vows of repentance and amendment. They will be invited by the same solemn occasion to call to mind the distinguished favors conferred on the American people in the general health which has been enjoyed, in the abundant fruits of the season, in the progress of the arts instrumental to their comfort, their prosperity, and their security, and in the victories which have so powerfully contributed to the defense and protection of our country, a devout thankfulness for all which ought to be mingled with their supplications to the Beneficent Parent of the Human Race that He would be graciously pleased to pardon all their offenses against Him; to support and animate them in the discharge of their respective duties; to continue to them the precious advantages flowing from political institutions so auspicious to their safety against dangers from abroad, to their tranquility at home, and to their liberties, civil and religious; and that He would in a special manner preside over the nation in its public councils and constituted authorities, giving wisdom to its measures and success to its arms in maintaining its rights and in overcoming all hostile designs and attempts against it; and, finally, that by inspiring the enemy with dispositions favorable to a just and reasonable peace its blessings may be speedily and happily restored.

Given at the city of Washington, the 16 day of November, 1814, and of the Independence of the United States the thirty-eighth.

JAMES MADISON[3]

Appendix D

By the President of the United States of America.

A PROCLAMATION.

Whereas a joint committee of both Houses of Congress has waited on the President of the United States and requested him to "recommend a day of public humiliation, prayer, and fasting to be observed by the people of the United States with religious solemnities and the offering of fervent supplications to Almighty God for the safety and welfare of these States, His blessings on their arms, and a speedy restoration of peace;" and

Whereas it is fit and becoming in all people at all times to acknowledge and revere the supreme government of God, to bow in humble submission to His chastisements, to confess and deplore their sins and transgressions in the full conviction that the fear of the Lord is the beginning of wisdom, and to pray with all fervency and contrition for the pardon of their past offenses and for a blessing upon their present and prospective action; and

Whereas when our own beloved country, once, by the blessing of God, united, prosperous, and happy, is now afflicted with faction and civil war, it is peculiarly fit for us to recognize the hand of God in this terrible visitation, and in sorrowful remembrance of our own faults and crimes as a nation and as individuals to humble ourselves before Him and to pray for His mercy—to pray that we may be spared further punishment, though most justly deserved; that our arms may be blessed and made effectual for the reestablishment of law, order, and peace throughout the wide extent of our country; and that the inestimable boon of civil and religious liberty, earned under His guidance and blessing by the labors and sufferings of our fathers, may be restored in all its original excellence:

Therefore I, Abraham Lincoln, President of the United States, do appoint the last Thursday in September next as a day of humiliation, prayer, and fasting for all the people of the nation. And I do earnestly recommend to all the people, and especially to all ministers and teachers of religion of all denominations and to all heads of families, to observe and keep that day according to their several creeds and modes of worship in all humility and with all religious solemnity, to the end that the united prayer of the nation may ascend to the Throne of Grace and bring down plentiful blessings upon our country.

In testimony whereof I have hereunto set my hand and caused the seal of the United States to be affixed, this 12th day of August, A.D. 1861, and of the Independence of the United States of America the eighty-sixth.

ABRAHAM LINCOLN.

By the President:

WILLIAM H. SEWARD, Secretary of State.[4]

APPENDIX E

By the President of the United States of America.

A PROCLAMATION.

Whereas the Senate of the United States, devoutly recognizing the supreme authority and just government of Almighty God in all the affair of men and of nations, has by a resolution requested the President to designate and set apart a day for national prayer and humiliation; and

Whereas it is the duty of nations as well as of men to own their dependence upon the overruling power of God, to confess their sins and transgressions in humble sorrow, yet with assured hope that genuine repentance will lead to mercy and pardon, and to recognize the sublime truth, announced in the Holy Scriptures and proven by all history, that those nations only are blessed whose God is the Lord;

And, insomuch as we know that by His divine law nations, like individuals, are subjected to punishments and chastisements in this world, may we not justly fear that the awful calamity of civil war which now desolates the land may be but a punishment inflicted upon us for our presumptuous sins, to the needful end of our national reformation as a whole people? We have been the recipients of the choicest bounties of Heaven; we have been preserved these many years in peace and prosperity; we have grown in numbers, wealth, and power as no other nation has ever grown. But we have forgotten God. We have forgotten the gracious hand which preserved us in peace and multiplied and enriched and strengthened us, and we have vainly imagined, in the deceitfulness of our hearts, that all these blessings were produced by some superior wisdom and virtue of our own. Intoxicated with unbroken success, we have become too self-sufficient to feel the necessity of redeeming and preserving grace, too proud to pray to the God that made us.

It behooves us, then, to humble ourselves before to be offended Power, to confess our national sins, and to pray for clemency and forgiveness.

Now, therefore, in compliance with the request, and fully concurring in the views of the Senate, I do by this my proclamation designate and set apart Thursday, the 30th day of April, 1863, as a day of national humiliation, fasting, and prayer. And I do hereby request all the people to abstain on that day from their ordinary secular pursuits, and to unite at their several places of public worship and their respective homes in keeping the day holy to the Lord and devoted to the humble discharge of the religious duties proper to that solemn occasion.

All this being done in sincerity and truth, let us then rest humbly in the hope authorized by the divine teachings that the united cry of the nation will be heard on high and answered with blessings no less than the pardon of our national sins and the restoration of our own divided and suffering country to its former happy condition of unity and peace.

In witness whereof I have hereunto set my hand and caused the seal of the United States to be affixed.

Done at the city of Washington, this 30th day of March, A.D. 1863, and of the Independence of the United States the eighty-seventh.

ABRAHAM LINCOLN.

By the President:
WILLIAM H. SEWARD, Secretary of State.[5]

APPENDIX F

By the President of the United States of America

A PROCLAMATION

Whereas the Senate and House of Representatives at their last session adopted a concurrent resolution which was approved on the 2d day of July instant and which was in the words following, namely:

That the President of the United States be requested to appoint a day for humiliation and prayer by the people of the United States; that he request his constitutional advisers at the head of the Executive Departments to unite with him as Chief Magistrate of the nation, at the city of Washington, and the members of Congress, and all magistrates, all civil, military, and naval officers, all soldiers, sailors, and marines, with all loyal and law-abiding people to convene at their usual places of worship, or wherever they may be, to confess and to repent of their manifold sins; to implore the compassion and forgiveness of the Almighty, that, if consistent with His will, the existing rebellion may be speedily suppressed and the supremacy of the Constitution and laws of the United States may be established throughout all the States; to implore Him, as the Supreme Ruler of the World, not to destroy us as a people, nor suffer us to be destroyed by the hostility or connivance of other nations or by obstinate adhesion to our own counsels, which may be in conflict with His eternal purposes, and to implore Him to enlighten the mind of the nation to know and do His will, humbly believing that it is in accordance with His will that our place should be maintained as a united people among the family of nations; to implore Him to grant to our armed defenders and the masses of the people that courage, power of resistance, and endurance necessary to secure that result to implore Him in His infinite goodness to soften the hearts, enlighten the minds, and quicken the consciences of those in rebellion, that they may lay down their arms and speedily return to their allegiance to the United States, that they may not be utterly destroyed, that the effusion of blood may be stayed, and that unity and fraternity may be restored and peace established throughout all our borders:

Now, therefore, I, Abraham Lincoln, president of the United States cordially concurring with the Congress of the United States in the penitential and pious sentiments expressed in the aforesaid resolution and heartily approving of the devotional design and purpose thereof, do hereby appoint the first Thursday of August next to be observed by the people of the United States as a day of national humiliation and prayer.

I do hereby further invite and request the heads of the Executive Departments of this Government, together with all legislators, all judges and magistrates, and all other persons exercising authority in the land, whether civil, military, or naval, and all soldiers, seamen, and marines in the national service, and all the other loyal and law-abiding people of the United States, to assemble in their preferred places of public worship on that day, and there and then to render to the almighty and merciful Ruler of the Universe such homages and such confessions and to offer to Him such supplications as the Congress of the United States have in their aforesaid resolution so solemnly, so earnestly, and so reverently recommended.

In testimony whereof I have hereunto set my hand and caused the seal of the United States to be affixed.

Done at the city of Washington, this 7th day of July, A.D. 1864, and of the Independence of the United States the eighty-ninth.

ABRAHAM LINCOLN.

By the President:
WILLIAM H. SEWARD, Secretary of State.[6]

APPENDIX G

Sample Fasting Questionnaire
(See page 99)

1. Have you ever fasted for a religious purpose?
   Yes   No

2. How often do you fast? (Please circle.)
   a. Weekly   b. Monthly   c. Yearly

3. What is the usual length of your fast?

4. When do you fast? (Please circle.)
   a. When God impresses you.
   b. When the pastor or other leader asks you.
   c. Other.

5. Have you ever fasted a week or more?
   Yes   No

If yes, how long?

6. What was your motive for fasting?   (Please circle.)
a. Lost souls.
b. Healing.
c. Financial need.
d. To find the will of God.
e. Personal repentance.
f. Mourning because of a death or tragedy.

7. Have you received the answers or the results you intended?
    Yes   No

8. Do you continue your daily work routine while you fast?
    Yes   No

9. Do you pray during the meal(s) you are fasting?
    Yes   No

10. Do you read the Bible during the fast?
    Yes   No

11. Do you drink liquids when you fast?
    Yes   No

If yes, please circle.
a.   Water
b.   Juice
c.   Soft drinks
d.   Coffee
e.   Tea
f.   Other

12. During and/or following a fast do you feel closer to God?
    Yes   No

13. During and/or following a fast are you more mentally alert?

Yes   No

14. During and/or following a fast have you ever had a vision?

Yes   No

15. During and/or following a fast have you ever had an unusual experience?

Yes   No

NOTES

Introduction

1. James Strong, *Strongs Exhaustive Concordance* p. 45, 90, 98 in the "Hebrew and Chaldee Dictionary."

2. Ibid., p. 50 in the "Greek Dictionary of the New Testament."

3. Friedrich Samuel Rothenberg "Fast," *The New International Dictionary of New Testament Theology.* 1, 611.

4. Strong, *Concordance.* p. 16 in the "Greek Dictionary of the New Testament"

5. Alfred Edersheim, *The Temple, Its Ministry and Services* p. 341.

6. "Fasts and Fasting," *The Oxford Dictionary of the Christian Church,* ed. F.L. Cross, p. 495.

7. Johannes Behm, "Nestis, nesteuo, nesteia," *Theological Dictionary of the New Testament,* pp. 926, 927; Rothenburg "Fast," p. 611, Moshe David Herr, *"Fasting and Fast Days,"* *Encyclopaedia Judaica,* p. 1194.

8. Harold Smith, *Fast Your Way to Health,* p. 84, citing J. Hastings, ed., "Fasting" *Encyclopedia of Religion and Ethics:* Floyd H. Ross, "Fast," *World Book Encyclopedia,* VII, p. 55.

9. Pierce Johnson, "Fasting as a Modern Discipline," *Religion in Life.* Autumn 1975, pp. 331-32.

10. Theodor H. Gaster, "Fasting" *Encyclopedia Americana* XI, p. 42.

11. Gaster, "Fasting," p. 42; Paul Martin, "The Benefits of Fasting" *Christian Century* p. 298.

12. Martin, "The Benefits of Fasting," p. 298; Johnson, "Fasting," p. 333.

13. Ross, "Fast," p. 55; Johnson, "Fasting" p. 332; Eric N. Rogers, *Fasting: The Phenomenon of Self-Denial.* pp. 89-96, 101ff.

14. Rogerts, *Fasting.* pp. 83-88, 97-100.

Chapter 1
The Pentateuch

1. Eric M. Rogers. Fasting *The Phenomenon of Self-Denial* p. 38

2. Merrill C. Tenney, *New Testament Survey.* p. 97.

3. J.P. Lewis, "*Fast, Fasting.*" The Zondervan Pictorial Encyclopedia of the Bible. II, p. 502.

4. Alfred Edersheim, *The Temple. Its Ministry and Services.* p.341.

5. Abraham Z. Idelsheim, *The Ceremonies of Judaism,* p. 21.

6. Yaacov Vainstein, *The Cycle of the Jewish Year,* p. 168.

7. Fred H. Wight, *Manners and Customs of Bible Lands,* p. 83.

Chapter 2
The Historical Books

1. George F. Moore, "Critical and Exegetical Commentary on Judges," *The International Critical Commentary.* pp. 412-443.

2. James Josiah Reeve, "Sacrifice," *The International Standard Bible Encyclopaedia.* IV, p. 2644.

3. Merrill F. Unger," Fast, Fasting" *Unger's Bible Dictionary.* p. 345.

4. M. Pierce Matheney, Jr., and Boy L. Honeycutt, Jr., "I Kings," *Broadman Bible Commentary,* vol. 3: *1 Samuel-Nehemiah,* p. 198.

5. James A. Montgomery, "The Books of Kings." *The International Critical Commentary.* p. 313.

6. Ibid, p. 330.

7. Matheney and Honeycutt, "1 Kings," p. 219.

8. David Alexander and Par Alexander, eds., *Eerdmans' Handbook to the Bible,* p. 308.

9. Idem.

10. Matheney and Honeycutt, "1 Kings," p. 472; Alexander and Alexander, *Handbook.* p. 309.

11. Matheney and Honeycutt, 1 Kings," p. 471.

Chapter 3
The Poetical and Wisdom Books

1. John I. Durham, "Psalms." *The Broadman Bible Commentary.* vol. 4: *Esther-Psalms*, p. 241.

Chapter 4
The Books of the Major Prophets

1. Franz Delitzsch, "Biblical Commentary on the Prophecies of Isaiah, II" *Commentaries on the Old Testament.* p. 385.

2 Ibid., p. 390.

3.Ibid., p. 393.

4. Carl Friedrich Keil, "Biblical Commentary on the Book of Daniel," *Biblical Commentary on the Old Testament. XXIII,* p. 408.

Chapter 5
The Books of the Minor Prophets

1. Julius A. Bewer, "Joel," *The International Critical Commentary,* in vol. *Micah*, p. 79; Carl Friedrich Keil, "Joel," *Biblical Commentary on the Old Testament,* Vol. 24: *The Twelve Minor Prophets*, p. 184.

2. Keil, "Joel," p. 184; Bewer, "Joel," p. 85; Alfred Erdersheim. *The Life and Times of Jesus the Messiah,* Book One, p. 662. See Deut. 24:5.

3. A.J. Glaze, Jr. "Jonah," *The Broadman Bible Commentary.* vol. 7: *Hosea-Malachi*: p. 174.

4. Ibid., pp. 175-177. See Jer. 18:8-10.

5. Carl Friedrich Keil, "Zechariah," *Biblical Commentary on the Old Testament,* vol. 25: *The Twelve Minor Prophets*, pp. 303-306.

6. John D.W. Watts, "Zechariah," *The Broadman Bible Commentary* vol. 7: *Hosea-Malachi*; pp. 331-332.

7. Keil, "Zechariah," p. 310. See Amos 2:6ff, 5:21ff; Hos. 6:4ff; Isa. 1:10ff; Mic. 2:1ff, 6:6ff; Jer.7:1ff; Ezek. 18:5ff. Hinckley G. Mitchell, "Zechariah," *"The International Critical Commentary,* vol.: *Haggai,* p. 201.

Chapter 6
The Intertestamental Period

1. Johannes Behm, "Nestis, nesteuo, nesteia," *Theological Dictionary of the New Testament*, pp. 928-929.
2. Joseph F. Wimmer, *Fasting in the New Testament*, p. 19; J.P. Lewis, "Fast, Fasting" *The Zondervan Pictoral Encyclopedia of the Bible*, p. 503.
3. Lewis, "Fast, Fasting" p. 503.
4. Wimmer, *Fasting*, p. 11-17.
5. Behm, "Nestis," p. 929.
6. Ibid, pp. 930-931.
7. Wimmer, *Fasting* pp. 23-27.
8. Ibid, pp. 27-30. See also *Eusebius' Ecclesiastical History*, pp. 67-70.

Chapter 7
The Gospels

1.The last two paragraphs are seen in Joseph F. Wimmer, *Fasting in the New Testament*, pp. 34-44 and R.V.G. Tasker, "The Gospel According to St. Matthew," *The Tyndale New Testament Commentaries*. pp. 52-56.
2. Wimmer, *Fasting*, p. 57 gives a detailed discussion regarding the history of the unity of the three.
3. Tasker "Matthew," p. 71; Wimmer, *Fasting*. p. 68. The Greek verb *apecho* was used in receipts to mean payment had been fully made.
4. Wimmer, *Fasting*, p. 76.
5. Ibid., p. 64.
6. Ibid., p. 70.
7. Ibid., p. 74.
8. Alfred Edersheim, *The Life and Times of Jesus the Messiah*, Book Three, p. 662.
9. Ezra P. Gould, "The Gospel of Mark." *The International Critical Commentary*, p. 45.
10. Ibid, p. 46.
11. Malcolm O. Tolbert, "Luke," *The Broadman Bible Commentary*, vol. 9: *Luke-John*, pp. 68-69. According to Tolbert, saying Jesus has a devil is a way of saying that He is crazy.
12. Alfred Plummer, "The Gospel According to St. Luke, *The International Critical Commentary*, pp. 417-418.

13. Edersheim, *Jesus the Messiah,* Book Four, p. 291.

14. Wimmer, *Fasting,* p. 81: "J. Blank notes that the background to v. 14a is to be found in the cultic *zaddiq*-sentence of the priests which presumably accompanied certain liturgical ceremonies at the gate of the Temple. Those who were declared 'just' were allowed to enter the Temple and worship there. Remnants of such a *Toraliturgie* are Ezek. 18:5-9; Pss. 15:1-5, 24:3-6; Isa. 33:14-16." From J. Blank, *Schriftauslegung in Theorie und Praxis* (Munich: Kosel-Verlag, 1969), p. 151; and W. Zimmerli, *Ezechial* (Neukirchen-Vluyn: Neukirchener Verlag, 1969), pp. 397-400.

15. Edersheim, *Jesus the Messiah,* Book Four p. 292.

16. Tasker, "Matthew," p. 167. *The Interpreter's Bible,* ed. George Arthur Buttrick p. 464 agrees with this view.

17. Harold J. Greenlee, *Introduction to New Testament Textual Criticism,* pp. 33-51.

18. Kurt Aland, et.al., eds., *The Greek New Testament,* pp. 66, 159.

19. Greenlee, *Textual Criticism,* p. 68. See Wimmer, *Fasting.* p. 77. Buttrick, *Interpreter's Bible,* p. 464 concurs with this.

Chapter 8
The New Testament Church and the Letters of Paul

1. Kurt Aland, et. al., eds., *The Greek New Testament,* p.456. See Joseph F. Wimmer, *Fasting in the New Testament.* p. 94.

2. T.C. Smith, "Acts." *The Broadman Bible Commentary,* vol. 10: *Acts-I Corinthians,* p. 131.

3. Aland, et al., *Greek New Testament,* p. 591.

4. R.V.G. Tasker, "The Gospel According to St. Matthew, *The Tyndale New Commentaries,* pp. 93, 164; Wimmer, *Fasting* p. 109; Alfred Plummer, "A Critical and Exegetical Commentary of the Second Epistle of St. Paul to the Corinthians," *The International Critical Commentary,* pp. 195, 328.

5. Wimmer, *Fasting,* p. 22.

Chapter 9
The Ante-Nicene Era

1. Geoffrey Wigoder, ed., "Fast," *The New Standard Jewish Encyclopedia,* p. 69; Abraham P. Bloch, *The Biblical and Historical Background of the Jewish Holy Days,* p. 244.

2. J.B. Lightfoot, *The Apostolic Fathers*, pp. 35-36, 97.

3. Ibid., pp. 123, 126.

4. Ibid., pp. 138, 139, 143, 150; in Lev. 23:29 ("cut off" may only mean excommunication).

5. Lightfoot, *Fathers*. pp. 168, 170, 177, 203-205.

6. Ibid., p. 253.

7. Ibid., p. 50.

8. George A. Maloney, *A Return to Fasting*, pp. 16-17. During the life of Justin Martyr fasting prepared one for baptism according to the Confessions and Letters of St. Augustine . . . ," *The Nicene and Post-Nicene Fathers*, I, p. 154.

9. Franklin Hall, *The Fasting Prayer*, p. 10.

10. Henry Bettenson, ed., *Documents of the Christian Church* p. 28.

11. Alexander Roberts and James Donaldson, eds, "Fathers of the Third Century," *The Ante-Nicene Fathers*, IV, VII, pp. 444-49.

12. Bettenson, *Documents*, p. 77; Joseph F. Wimmer, *Fasting in the New Testament*, p. 52.

13. Roberts and Donaldson, "*Fathers*," VII, pp. 444-449.

14. Ibid., VIII, p. 164, 613; Allan Men zies, ed., The Ante-Nicene Fathers, X, p. 161.

15. Roberts and Donaldson, "*Fathers*," VIII, p. 44.

16. Kenneth Scott Latourette, *A History of Christianity*, p.137; Franz Delitzsch, "Biblical Commentary on the Prophecies of Isaiah," *Commentaries in the Old Testament*, II, p. 386.

17. *Eusebius' Ecclesiastical History*, pp. 106, 108, 186-187.

18. Ibid., pp. 22, 54 in "A Historical View of the Council of Nice."

19. Ibid., pp. 207-211.

20. Ibid., p. 222, 232, 375-377

Chapter 10
The Nicene and Post-Nicene Eras

1. Philip Schaff and Henry Wace, eds. "St. Basil: Letters and Select Works" *The Nicene and Post-Nicene Fathers*, VIII, p. lxi.

2. Philip Schaff and Henry Wace, eds., "St. Ambrose: Select Works and Letters," *The Nicene and Post-Nicene Fathers*, X, p. 459.

3. Philip Schaff, ed., "St. Chrysostom: Homilies on the Gospel of Saint Matthew," *The Nicene and Post-Nicene Fathers*, X, p. 80.

4. Philip Schaff and Henry Wace, eds., "St. Jerome: Letters and Select Works," *The Nicene and Post-Nicene Fathers*, VI, pp. 246-247, 392, 398-400.

5. Philip Schaff, ed., "The Confessions and Letters of St. Augustine...," *The Nicene and Post-Nicene Fathers*. I, p. 154; "Saint Augustine: Anti-Pelagian Writings," *The Nicene and Post-Nicene Fathers*, V, p. 164.

6. Joseph F. Wimmer, *Fasting in the New Testament*, p. 52 footnote 5.

7. Ibid., p. 52 footnote 6.

8. Ibid., p. 31; Henry Gallus, *Sanctify a Fast*, pp. 10-11.

Chapter 11
The Medieval Era

1. Merrill F. Unger, "Fast, Fasting" *Unger's Bible Dictionary*, p. 346; Eric N. Rogers, *Fasting: The Phenomenon of Self-Denial*, p. 43.

2. Rogers, *Fasting*, p. 42; Henry Bettenson, *Documents of the Christian Church*, pp. 120-130, 162; Philip Schaff and Henry Wace, eds., "Theodoret, Jerome, Gennadius, Rufinus: Historical Writings, etc.," *The Nicene and Post-Nicene Fathers*, III, p. 393; Justo L. Gonzalez, *A History of Christian Thought*, II, p. 97; Abraham P. Bloch, *The Biblical and Historical Background of the Jewish Holy Days*, p. 254.

3. George A. Maloney, *A Return to Fasting*, p. 7; Gonzalez, *Christian Thought*, p. 136; Rogers, *Fasting*, pp. 44-45,

Chapter 12
The Reformation and Post-Reformation Eras

1. Eric N. Rogers, *Fasting: The Phenomenon of Self-Denial*, p. 46; Thomas W. Klewin, "Fasting Can Improve Your Life," *These Times*, September 1979, pp. 10-11; J. Harold Smith, *Fast Your Way to Health*, p. 87; Ray W. Johnson, "New Dimension of Faith," *Christian Life*. October 1963, p. 42.

2. David R. Smith, *Fasting: A Neglected Discipline*, p. 50.

3. Williston Walker, *A History of the Christian Church* p. 373; Ray W. Johnson, "New Dimension," p. 42.

4. John Calvin, *Institutes of the Christian Religion*, II, pp. 424-427.

5. Matthew Henry, *Matthew Henry's Commentary in One Volume*, pp. 1230, 1293.

6. Walker, *History,* pp. 465-466 Gordon Chilvers, "A Hunger for Righteousness," *The Christian Reader*, March/April 1978, pp. 46-47.

7. Rogers, *Fasting*, p. 47; Derek Prince, *Shaping History Through Prayer and Fasting*, p. 116.

8. Henry Gallus, *Sanctify a Fast*, pp. 11, 17, 29.

9. Arthur Wallis, *God's Chosen Fast*, pp. 34-35.

10. David R. Smith, *Fasting*, p. 46, from Jonathan Edwards, *The Life of David Brainerd*, p. 26; J. Harold Smith, *Fast Your Way*, p. 89; Ray W. Johnson, *New Dimension*, p. 42.

11. David R. Smith, *Fasting*, p. 41, 50, (quoted from E.M. Bounds in *Power Through Prayer*, p. 31); I. Harold Smith, *Fast Your Way*. p. 89.

12. Calvin, *Institutes*, pp. 421-423.

13. Rogers, *Fasting*, pp. 71, 73; David R. Smith, *Fasting*, p. 35.

14. Idem.

15. Rogers, *Fasting*, pp. 72-74.

16. Ibid., p. 47.

17. Henry K. Rowe, "Fast-day," *The New Schaff-Herzog Encyclopedia*, IV, p. 280.

18. Rogers, *Fasting*, p. 72

19. Rowe, "Fast Day," p. 280. Prince, *Shaping History,* has a detailed account on pp. 136-137.

20. *Shaping History,* Prince, pp. 136-137

21. Rogers, *Fasting,* pp. 74-75; Prince, *Shaping History*, pp. 138-139.

22. Prince, *Shaping History*, pp. 141-142.

23. Ibid., pp. 142-143.

24. Rogers, *Fasting*, p. 76.

Chapter 13
The Modern Era

1. Eric N. Rogers, *Fasting: The Phenomenon of Self-Denial,* pp. 75-76; Henry K. Rowe, "Fast Day," *The New Schaff-Herzog Encyclopedia*, IV, p. 280.

2. Moshe David Herr, "Fasting and Fast Days," *Encyclopaedia Judaica*, p. 1195; Rogers, *Fasting*, pp. 46-48, 50.

3. Hans Achelis, "Fasting," *The New Schaff-Herzog Encyclopedia*, IV, pp. 283-284.

4. Ray W. Johnson, "New Dimensions of Faith," *Christian Life,* October 1963, p. 42; Derek Prince, *Shaping History Through Prayer and Fasting,* pp. 58-76; Henry Gallus, *Sanctify a Fast,* p. 28; David R. Smith, *Fasting: A Neglected Discipline,* p. 55; "The Benefits of Prayer and Fasting: An Interview with Ja Shil Choi, Seoul, Korea," *Pentecostal Evangel,* October 29, 1978, p. 8.

5. "The Benefits of Prayer and Fasting: An Interview with Ja Shil Choi, Seoul, Korea," p. 8; F Vilgoen, "What the Bible Says About Fasting," *Vision,* August-September 1979, p. 11 in Vision Supplement; Franklin Hall, *The Fasting Prayer,* pp. 13, 16; Gordon Lindsay, *Prayer and Fasting,* p. 7; David R. Smith, *Fasting,* pp. 45-56; Arthur Wallis, *God's Chosen Fast,* pp. 36-70; J. Harold Smith, *Fast Your Way to Health,* p. 9.

6. Gallus, *Sanctify,* p. 6; James Lee Beall, *The Adventure of Fasting,* p.11; Joseph F. Wimmer, *Fasting in the New Testament,* p. 117.

7. Maloney, p. 7.

Appendices

1. Derek Prince, *Shaping History Through Fasting,* pp. 138-139.

2. Prepared under the direction of the Joint Committee on Printing, of the House and Senate, Pursuant to an Act of the Fifty-second Congress of the United States, *Messages and Papers of the Presidents* (New York: Bureau of National Literature, Inc., 1897), I, pp. 258-260.

3. Ibid., vol. II, p. 543

4. Ibid., vol. VII, pp. 3237-3238

5. Ibid., vol. VII, pp. 3365-3366

6. Ibid., vol. VII, pp. 3422-3423

SELECTED BIBLIOGRAPHY

Achelis, Hans. "Fasting," *The New Schaff-Herzog Encyclopedia*, vol. IV. Edited by Samuel Macauley Jackson. Grand Rapids: Baker Book House, 1967.

Aland, Kurt; Black, Matthew; Martini, Carlo M.; Metzger, Bruce M.; and Wikgren, Allen, eds. *The Greek New Testament*, 3rd ed. New York: American Bible Society, 1975.

Alexander, David, and Alexander, Pat, eds. *Eerdmans' Handbook to the Bible*. Grand Rapids: Wm. B. Eerdmans Publishing Company, 1973.

Arndt, William, F., and Gingrich, R. Wilbur. *A Greek-English Lexicon of New Testament and Other Early Christian Literature.* 2nd ed. Chicago: The University of Chicago Press, 1979.

Beall, James Lee. *The Adventure of Fasting*. Old Tappan, New Jersey: Fleming H. Revell Company, 1974.

Behm, Johannes. "Nestis, nesteuo, nesteia." *Theological Dictionary of the New Testament,* vol. IV. Edited by Gerhard Kittel. Translated and edited by Geoffrey W. Bromiley. Grand Rapids: Wm. B. Eerdmans Publishing Company, 1967.

Bettenson, Henry, ed. *Documents of the Christian Church.* 2nd ed. London: Oxford University Press, 1981.

Bewer, Julius A. "Joel" in *Micah, Zephaniah, Nahum, Habakkuk, Obadiah and Joel*, The International Critical Commentary. Edited by Samuel Rolles Driver, Alfred Plummer and Charles Augustus Briggs. Edinburgh: T. & T. Clark, 1965.

Bloch, Abraham P. *The Biblical and Historical Background of the Jewish Holy Days.* New York: Ktav Publishing House, Inc., 1978.

Buttrick, George Arthur, ed. *The Interpreter's Bible.* 12 vols, New York: Abingdon-Cokesbury Press, 1951.

Calvin, John. *Institutes of the Christian Religion*, vol. II. Philadelphia: Presbyterian Board of Publication, 1909.

Chilvers, Gordon. "A Hunger for Righteousness." *The Christian Reader*, March/April 1987, pp. 45-48.

Delitzsch, Franz. *Biblical Commentary on the Prophecies of Isaiah, II.* Commentaries on the Old Testament, 3rd ed. Translated by James Martin. Grand Rapids: Wm. B. Eerdmans Publishing Company, 1965.

Durham, John I. "Psalms" in *Esther-Psalms*. The Broadman Bible Commentary. Gen. ed. Clifton J. Allen. Nashville: Broadman Press, 1971.

Edersheim, Alfred, *The Life and Times of Jesus the Messiah.* Grand Rapids: Wm. B.
     Eerdmans Publishing Company, 1972. *The Temple, Its Ministry and
     Services.* Grand Rapids: Wm. B. Eerdmans Publishing Company, 1972.

Eusebius' Ecclesiastical History. Translated by Christian Frederick Cruse. Grand
     Rapids: Baker Book House, 1977.

"Fasts and Fasting." *The Oxford Dictionary of the Christian Church.* Edited by
     F.L. Cross. London: Oxford University Press, 1958.

Gallus, Henry. *Sanctify a Fast.* Blenheim, New Zealand: A Back-to-the-Bible
     Publication, 1954.

Gaster, Theodor H. "Fasting." *Encyclopedia Americana,* vol. VI. New York:
     Americana Corporation, 1977.

Glaze, A.J., Jr. "Jonah" in *Hosea-Malachi,* The Broadman Bible Commentary, vol. VII.
     Gen. Ed. Clifton J. Allen, Nashville: Broadman Press, 1972.

Gonzalez, Justo, L. *A History of Christian Thought,* vol. II. Nashville: Abingdon
     Press, 1971.

Gould, Ezra P. *The Gospel of Mark,* The International Critical Commentary. Edited by
     Samuel Rolles Driver, Alfred Plummer and Charles Augustus Briggs.
     Edinburgh: T. & T. Clark, 1961.

Greenlee, J. Harold. *Introduction to New Testament Textual Criticism.* Grand
     Rapids: Wm. B. Eerdmans Publishing Company, 1964.

Hall, Franklin. *The Fasting Prayer.* 2nd ed. San Diego: Franklin Hall, 1954.

Hamrick, Emmett Willard. "Ezra, Nehemiah" in *1 Samuel-Nehemiah,* The Broadman
     Bible Commentary, vol. III. Gen. Ed. Clifton J. Allen. Nashville: Broadman
     Press, 1970.

Henry Matthew. *Matthew Henry's Commentary in One Volume.* Grand Rapids:
     Zondervan Publishing House, 1961.

Herr, Moshe David. "Fasting and Fast Days." *Encyclopaedia Judaica,* vol. VI.
     Editors in chief Cecil Roth and Geoffrey Wigoder. Jerusalem: Keter
     Publishing House Ltd., 1971.

Idelsohn, Abraham Z. *The Ceremonies of Judaism.* Cincinnati: The National
     Federation of Temple Brotherhoods, 1929.

Johnson, Pierce. "Fasting a Modern Discipline." *Religion in Life,* Autumn 1975, pp.
     331-337.

Johnson, Ray W. "New Dimension of Faith." *Christian Life,* October 1963, pp. 41-
     42.

Keil, Carl Friedrich. *Biblical Commentary on the Book of Daniel,* Biblical
    Commentary on the Old Testament, vol. XXIII. Edited by C.F. Keil and Franz
    Delitzsch. Translated by M.G. Easton. Grand Rapids: Wm. B. Eerdmans
    Publishing Company, 1965.

————— "Joel" in *The Twelve Minor Prophets, I,* Biblical Commentary on the Old
    Testament, vol. XXIV. Edited by C.F. Keil and Franz Delitzsch. Translated by
    James Martin. Grand Rapids: Wm. B. Eerdmans Publishing Company,
    1961.

————— "Zechariah" in *The Twelve Minor Prophets,* II Biblical Commentary on the
    Old Testament, vol. XV. Edited by C.F. Keil and Franz Delitzsch. Translated
    by James Martin. Grand Rapids: Wm. B. Eerdmans Publishing Company,
    1961.

Klewin, Thomas W. "Fasting Can Improve Your Life." *These Times,* September 1979,
    pp. 10-11.

Latourette, Kenneth Scott. *A History of Christianity.* New York: Harper and Row,
    1953

Lewis, J.P. "Fast, Fasting." *The Zondervan Pictorial Encyclopedia of the Bible.*
    Gen. Ed. Merrill C. Tenney. Grand Rapids: Zondervan Publishing House,
    1975.

Lightfoot, J.B. *The Apostolic Fathers.* Edited by J.R. Harmer. Grand Rapids: Baker
    Book House, 1976.

Lindsay, Gordon. *Prayer and Fasting.* Dallas: Christ for the Nations, 1972.

Maloney, George A. *A Return to Fasting.* Pecos, New Mexico:Dove Publications,
    1974.

Martin, Paul. "The Benefits of Fasting." *Christian Century.* Ann Arbor, Michigan:
    University Microfilms, March 30, 1977, p. 298.

Matheney, M. Pierce, Jr. and Honeycutt, Roy L., Jr. "I Kings" in *I Samuel-Nehemiah,*
    Broadman Bible Commentary, vol. III. Gen. Ed. Clifton J. Allen. Nashville:
    Broadman Press, 1970.

Menzies, Allan, ed. *The Ante-Nicene Fathers,* vol. X. 5th ed. Translated by Andrew
    Rutherford. Grand Rapids: Wm. B. Eerdmans Publishing Company, 1965.

Milgrom, Jacob. "Fasting and Fast Days." *Encyclopaedia Judaica,* vol. VI. Editors
    in chief Cecil Roth and Geoffrey Wigoder, Jerusalem: Keter Publishing House
    Ltd., 1971.

Mitchell, Hinckley G. "Zechariah" in *Haggai, Zechariah, Malachi and Jonah,* The
    International Critical Commentary. Edited by Samuel Rolles Driver, Alfred
    Plummer and Charles Augustus Briggs. Edinburgh: T. & T. Clack, 1961.

Montgomery, James A. *The Books of Kings.* The International Critical Commentary. Edited by Henry Snyder Gehman Edinburgh: T. & T. Clark, 1960.

Moore, George F. *Critical and Exegetical Commentary on Judges,* The International Critical Commentary. Edited by Samuel Rolles Driver, Alfred Plummer and Charles Augustus Briggs. Edinburgh: T. & T. Clark, 1958.

Plummer, Alfred. *A Critical and Exegetical Commentary of the Second Epistle of St. Paul to the Corinthians. The International* Critical Commentary. Edited by Samuel Rolles Driver, Alfred Plummer and Charles Augustus Briggs. Edinburgh: T. & T. Clark, 1960.

———— *The Gospel According to S. Luke*, The International Critical Commentary. 5th ed. Edited by Samuel Rolles Driver, Alfred Plummer and Charles Augustus Briggs.Edinburgh: T. & T. Clark, 1960.

Prince, Derek. *Shaping History Through Prayer and Fasting.* Old Tappan, New Jersey: Fleming H. Revell Company, 1973.

Reeve, James Josiah. "Sacrifice." *The International Standard Bible Encyclopedia,* vol. IV. Gen ed. James Orr. Grand Rapids: Wm. B. Eerdmans Publishing Company, 1956.

Roberts, Alexander and Donaldson, James, eds. *Fathers of the Third Century,* The Ante-Nicene Fathers, vol. VI. Translated by S. Thelwall. Grand Rapids: Wm. B. Eerdmans Publishing Company, 1969.

————*Fathers of the Third and Fourth Centuries.* The Ante-Nicene Fathers, vol. VIII. Grand Rapids: Wm. B. Eerdmans Publishing Company, 1971.

Rogers, Eric N. Fasting: *The Phenomenon of Self-Denial.* Nashville: Thomas Nelson Inc., Publishers, 1976.

Ross, Floyd H. "Fast." *World Book Encyclopedia*, vol VII. Chicago: Field Enterprises Educational Corporation, 1972.

Rothenberg, Friedrich Samuel. "Fast." *The New International Dictionary of New Testament Theology,* vol. I. Gen. Ed. Colin Brown. Grand Rapids: Zondervan Publishing House, 1975.

Rowe, Henry K. "Fast-day." *The New Schaff-Herzog Encyclopedia,* vol. IV. Edited by Samuel Macauley Jackson. Grand Rapids: Baker Book House, 1967.

Schaff Philip, ed. *Saint Augustine Anti-Pelagian Writings,* The Nicene and Post-Nicene Fathers, vol V. Translated by Peter Holmes, Robert Ernest Wallis, Benjamin B. Warfield. Grand Rapids: Wm. B. Eerdmans Publishing Company, 1956.

———— *Saint Chrysostom: Homilies on the Gospel of Saint Matthew*, The Nicene and Post-Nicene Fathers, vol. X, First Series. Translated by George Prevost. Grand Rapids: Wm. B. Eerdmans Publishing Company, 1969.

———— *The Confessions and Letters of St. Augustine, With a Sketch of His Life and Work,* The Nicene and Post-Nicene Fathers, vol. I. First Series. Grand Rapids: Wm. B. Eerdmans Publishing Company, 1956.

Schaff, Philip and Wace, Henry, eds. *St. Ambrose: Select Works and Letters.* The Nicene and Post-Nicene Fathers, vol. X. Second Series. Translated by H. De Romestin, E. De Romestin and H.T.F. Duckworth. Grand Rapids: Wm. B. Eerdmans Publishing Company, 1955.

———— *St. Basil: Letters and Select Works.* The Nicene and Post-Nicene Fathers, vol. VIII Second Series. Translated by Blomfield Jackson. Grand Rapids: Wm. B. Eerdmans Publishing Company, 1968.

————*St. Jerome: Letters and Select Works,* The Nicene and Post-Nicene Fathers vol. VI. Second Series. Translated by W.H. Fremantle, G. Lewis and W.G. Martley. Grand Rapids: Wm. B. Eerdmans Publishing Company, 1954.

———— *Theodoret, Jerome, Gennadius, Rufinus: Historical Writings, etc,* The Nicene and Post-Nicene Fathers, vol III. Second Series. Grand Rapids: Wm. B. Eerdmans Publishing Company, 1969.

Smith, David R. *Fasting: A Neglected Discipline.* Fort Washington, PA: Christian Literature Crusade, 1954.

Smith, Henry Preserved. *The Books of Samuel,* The International Critical Commentary. Edited by Samuel Rolles Driver, Alfred Plummer and Charles Augustus Briggs. Edinburgh: T. & T. Clark, 1961.

Smith, J. Harold. *Fast Your Way to Health.* Nashville: Thomas Nelson Publishers, 1979.

Smith, T.C. "Acts" in *Acts-I Corinthians,* The Broadman Bible Commentary, vol. X. Gen. Ed. Clifton J. Allen. Nashville: Broadman Press, 1970.

Strong, James. S., "Fast." *Strong's Exhaustive Concordance.* Nashville: Regal Publishers, Inc., n.d.

Tasker, R.V.G. *The Gospel According to St. Matthew,* The Tyndale New Testament Commentaries. Grand Rapids: Wm. B. Eerdmans Publishing Company 1981.

Tenney, Merrill C. *New Testament Survey.* Grand Rapids: Wm. B. Eerdmans Publishing Company, 1961.

"The Benefits of Prayer and Fasting: an Interview with Ja Shil Choi, Seoul, Korea." Pentecostal Evangel, October 29, 1978, pp. 6-8.

Tolbert, Malcolm O. "Luke" in *Luke-John,* The Broadman Bible Commentary, vol. IX. Gen. Ed. Clifton J. Allen. Nashville: Broadman Press, 1970.

Unger, Merrill F. "Fast, Fasting." *Unger's Bible Dictionary.* Chicago: Moody Press, 1966.

Vainstein, Yaacov. *The Cycle of the Jewish Year.* 2nd rev. and enlargeded. Jerusalem: The World Zionist Organization, 1964.

Vilgoen, F. "What the Bible Says About Fasting." *Vision,* August-September 1979, p. 11 in Vision Supplement.

Walker, Williston. *A History of the Christian Church.* 3rd ed. New York: Charles Scribner's Sons, 1970.

Wallis, Arthur. *God's Chosen Fast.* Fort Washington, PA: Christian Literature Crusade, 1972.

Watts, John D.W. "Zechariah" in *Hosea-Malachi*, the Broadman Bible Commentary, vol. VII. Gen. Ed. Clifton J. Allen. Nashville: Broadman Press, 1972.

Wight, Fred H. *Manners and Customs of Bible Lands.* Chicago: Moody Press, 1953.

Wigoder, Geoffrey, ed. "Fast." *The New Standard Jewish Encyclopedia.* 5th ed. Garden City, New York: Doubleday and Company, Inc., 1977.

Wimmer, Joseph F. *Fasting in the New Testament.* New York: Paulist Press, 1982.